INTERNET-LINKED

Usborne
The World of
Ballet

Judy Tatchell
Designed by Ruth Russell
Edited by Lisa Miles
Illustrations by Evie Safarewicz and Guy Smith
Studio photography by Bill Cooper and Tony McConnell
Cover design by Andrea Slane

Contents

Consultants

Nicola Katrak, former Principal with Sadler's Wells Royal Ballet
Sue Manville, LRAD
David Bintley, choreographer
Amanda Eyles, dance notator with the English National Ballet
The Language of Dance Centre, London
Amanda Barlow, design consultant

Ballet steps demonstrated by members of The Birmingham Royal Ballet
(Lee Fisher, Elizabeth Gray, Duncan de Gruchy, Toby Norman-Wright, Reiko Miura and Rachel Peppin)

Produced in association with The Birmingham Royal Ballet

The art of ballet

The world of ballet is a fascinating one. People everywhere, whether they are dancers, spectators or both, can enjoy it. Unlike other forms of dance, such as folk dancing or dancing at social occasions, ballet is especially designed to be watched by an audience, so that hundreds of people can join in the experience. The dancers do not perform solely for their own pleasure. They aim to communicate feelings, ideas, stories and shapes to the spectators, without whom ballet would have little point.

This costume was designed for a ballet in the early 17th century.

What is ballet?

The word "ballet" refers to a specific dance technique, which has evolved over the last 350 years. At a ballet, you will see a dance performance, which takes place in a theatrical setting. Movement, music and design are brought together to create a show for the spectators. The dancers don't need words to communicate with their audience.

Each company of dancers has many different ballets in its repertory. Some have been danced repeatedly for up to 150 years by companies all over the world. Others are brand new and are created for a particular company.

Darcey Bussell and Irek Mukhamedov of The Royal Ballet, performing spectacular leaps from *La Bayadère*.

Why do people watch ballet?

People watch ballet for all sorts of reasons. It is exciting to go to the theatre and see a live performance. Watching ballet is a way of escaping from everyday life into a world of wonder and spectacle. It is a form of entertainment that appeals directly to people's emotions with a fusion of dance, music and art. To watch ballet is an opportunity to marvel at the achievements of the human body, as the dancers show their physical and dramatic skill.

Internet link
For a link to a website with photos and information about Irek Mukhamedov, go to **www.usborne-quicklinks.com**

Ballet technique

Much of the technique that today's dancers use has evolved from a style that developed in France during the 17th century. Most ballet steps have French names because of this. You can find out how to pronounce some of these on page 63.

One of the important basic principles is the turn-out of the leg from the hip. This enhances the line of the leg and increases the dancer's range of movement. Posture is also very important. Dancers should look graceful and elegant and they hold their bodies in such a way as to achieve this.

The dancers stretch up and out, moving to match the rhythm and mood of the music. To appear weightless, females dance on *pointe* – performing steps on the very tips of their toes, with help from stiffened shoes. To appear to defy gravity, men lift their women partners high in the air and both men and women perform leaps and jumps. Landings are quiet and soft, to make the jumps appear effortless.

A dancer must have a good sense of balance and be supple and loose. Many movements are amazing in the speed and skill that they require. Over the years, costumes have become lighter and easier to dance in.

The arms are curved.

The back and head are held erect.

The legs are turned out from the hip.

The feet are always pointed to lengthen the line of the leg.

Internet link
For a link to a website where you can watch a video clip of Darcey Bussell dancing and find out more about her, visit **www.usborne-quicklinks.com**

Ballet today

In the 19th century, national dances from around the world were often included in ballets. In the 20th century, tap, jazz and ethnic dance styles have also had a big influence. People who create ballets, called choreographers, don't always stick to the traditional technique. They often borrow movements from other dance styles, or they may invent their own.

Today, ballet is a truly international art form, with top companies based all over the world. Companies are often on tour and dancers may move frequently from company to company. Their art is one of the hardest dance techniques to master, and that is why dancers have to train for many years before they are ready to dance professionally.

THE BIRMINGHAM ROYAL BALLET & THE STUTTGART BALLET
Summer tour

It is a good opportunity to see top companies if they are on tour near your home.

Watching ballet

The story or idea behind the ballet is usually described in the programme.

On stage or on television, you can see several different kinds of ballet. Story ballets, which are usually split into several sections, or acts, follow the adventures of different characters. Ballets with no story, but which set a scene or convey a certain mood or idea, are called theme ballets. Abstract ballets display the skill of dancing for its own sake. Most theme and abstract ballets are just one act long.

At a performance, a pair of opera glasses will help you to see clearly.

Agnes Oaks and Thomas Edur of the English National Ballet dance a *pas de deux* from *Swan Lake*.

During a performance

When the auditorium lights dim at the start of a performance, there may be a piece of music called an overture before the curtain rises. This sets the atmosphere and might introduce music which matches the different characters who are about to appear. Once the curtain is up, the ballet may include any or all of the types of dances listed here.

Crowd scenes help to describe the setting of the story. The dancers' costumes and their style of movement provide clues.

Large group dances are danced by a team called the *corps de ballet*. They make floor patterns on the stage and usually move identically. There may also be **small group dances**, such as a *pas de trois* (a threesome).

Pas de deux are duets. In a story ballet, they often show the relationship between the hero and heroine.

Solos are performed by the leading dancers and may show the characters' feelings. Solos are usually technically difficult.

Mime scenes in some story ballets use gestures to show what is happening, without much actual dancing. If performed well, the meaning is usually obvious.

Divertissements are dances which do not move the story along, but which are just enjoyable to watch. They are often contained in story ballets.

A ***tableau*** is a frozen picture made by the dancers at the end of some ballets. They pose in a group as the curtain falls, for a striking ending.

Choosing a ballet

The most exciting way to see ballet is live on stage. Watching it on television or video has less atmosphere, although close-ups show the dancers' technique clearly. Most companies present a long story ballet or a set of shorter, one-act ballets. A set of three one-act ballets, called a triple bill, allows you to see contrasting styles.

Most of the famous ballets from the early 19th century are sad stories about spirits or ghosts. Ballets from this period, such as *Giselle* and *La Sylphide*, are often called Romantic ballets.

During the late 19th century, grand, spectacular story ballets were made up. These are often called Classical ballets, because they display very pure, or "classical", technique in ballet terms.

Most abstract and theme ballets were made in the 20th century, as well as new story ballets.

The picture above is from *The Sleeping Beauty*. Classical productions, such as this one by The Birmingham Royal Ballet, are usually lavish, with large casts and wonderful costumes and scenery.

Darcey Bussell and Zoltan Solymosi of The Royal Ballet in *Elite Syncopations*, a 20th century theme ballet, based on ragtime music.

Ricardo Bustamante of the American Ballet Theatre in *La Bayadère*, a 19th century ballet.

A scene from The Northern Ballet Theatre's production of *Giselle*, a Romantic ballet.

Choosing a seat

All auditoriums are different but this general layout might help you to choose a seat. A ballet is designed to be seen from the middle of the auditorium, so seats here are often more expensive than those at the side. Seats high up at the back are usually the cheapest. You may miss details but you will get a good view of patterns made by groups of dancers.

- Seats at the top and sides are the cheapest. Ask for seats as near the middle as possible.
- These seats give the best view, so they are the most expensive.
- You may not be able to see the whole stage from the sides near the front.
- If the front seats are low, you may not be able to see the dancers' feet.

How ballets tell stories

There are no words in ballets to tell the story, so the best way to make sure you understand what is going on is to find out the story in advance. You could try your local library or ask the ballet company's education department for a story guide. Even if you don't know the story, ballets use body language, costume, scenery, music and dance style to show what is happening.

This costume, worn by Cinderella, looks magical and fairy-like.

Romeo and Juliet
Swan Lake
Coppélia
The Nutcracker
La Sylphide
Giselle
The Firebird
Manon
La Fille Mal Gardée

The stories of these ballets, among others, are told on pages 56-58 in this book.

Samira Saidi of The Birmingham Royal Ballet.

Clues in the costume

Characters' costumes, makeup and hairstyles can tell you a lot about them. You can tell whether they are rich or poor, young or old, and what they do for a living. Some costumes can tell you what sort of person the character is. A dark, drab costume, for instance, might imply that the person is solemn or unhappy. A pure white costume often suggests purity and innocence.

The pictures on this page show how body language can be combined with costume to tell you about a character. Clues such as these might help you to understand the flow of a story, even if you don't pick up on every detail.

The doll from *Petrushka* wears a simple, bright costume. This helps to show her uncomplicated nature. Her movements are those of a puppet and her makeup gives her a doll-like face.

Sherilyn Kennedy of The Birmingham Royal Ballet.

The pictures above show Darcey Bussell in *Manon*. To start with she is wealthy and sophisticated. Later, she is a poor, sick convict. Her hair, clothes and makeup reflect this change dramatically.

The Snow Queen's brittle, cold-looking costume suggests a hard, icy cruelty. Her stare is cold and arrogant.

The costume, makeup and aggressive pose of the wizard Kostchei from *The Firebird* make him appear grotesque and very threatening. His crown shows that he is a powerful character.

David Drew of The Royal Ballet.

Clues in the scenery

The scenery provides information about where the story takes place. The style of lighting helps to set the mood. In the scenery shown here, the cold shades and the stark, silhouetted shapes create a spooky atmosphere.

This village scenery looks homely and cheerful. The lighting is warm, to show a summer's day. The clean brightness of the scene is idealistic rather than realistic. The atmosphere suggests that this scene in the ballet is probably light-hearted.

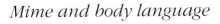

This palace interior is grand and imposing. The shadowy nooks and crannies suggest intrigue. The gloomy shades and huge pillars and stairways look threatening, so the story of this ballet is probably a tragedy.

Mime and body language

In the 19th century, ballets contained scenes between dances, during which the story was told using mimed gestures. Today, mime in ballet consists of a mixture of natural body language and some of these earlier, more stylized, mimed gestures. Many of these gestures are obvious, for instance, pointing to the eyes (to see), ears (to hear), mouth (to speak) or heart (to love). Some gestures are more obscure.

Along the bottom of the page are some of the mimed gestures you can still see in today's versions of Classical and Romantic ballets. The gestures used in later ballets are usually fairly obvious. For instance, the scene on the left from *The Taming of the Shrew*, was choreographed by John Cranko in 1969. The dancers are using a combination of gesture, facial expression and body language to show that they are having a fight.

Married ★   Read ★   Death ★   Promise ★   Please ★   Why? ★   Afraid ★

Early nineteenth century ballet

In the early 19th century, an artistic movement called Romanticism developed. The Romantic movement aimed to stir people's feelings, rather than just gain their admiration for the technical quality of its art. Painting, music and writing were all changed by this. Ballet was also affected and during the 1830s and 40s, the Romantic ballet style developed.

Romantic art was designed to appeal to people's emotions.

Romantic ballet themes

Most themes for Romantic ballets are escapist. This means that they have an unreal or fantasy element that makes the audience forget their everyday lives. For this reason, Romantic ballets often have two locations: a real place, and a supernatural world of spirits or magic.

This is Count Albrecht, who breaks Giselle's heart.

Dance style

In the supernatural scenes, the dancers jump high, as if they are flying. The male partner lifts the female to enhance the floating effect. The footwork is silent and the female dancers pose on *pointe* as if they are weightless. The arms are often held with delicately crossed wrists. In the real-life scenes, the technique often includes fast footwork and low jumps. Sometimes you can spot a folk dance influence, as in the Scottish reels in *La Sylphide*.

Group dances for the *corps de ballet* became more important in Romantic ballets. For the first time, the *corps de ballet* moved as one, giving the group more impact. Scenes where they are dressed in white to resemble spirits are sometimes known as "white acts".

Lisa Cullum and Bart de Block in a supernatural scene from the Berlin Ballet's production of *Giselle*.

Bart de Block of the Berlin Ballet.

Internet link
For a link to a website where you can find out more about Marie Taglioni, go to
www.usborne-quicklinks.com

Music for ballet

Romantic ballet music helps to describe the story's atmosphere. Before this period, most ballet music just marked out the rhythm in a way that was pleasant to listen to. The composer of the music for *Giselle*, Adolphe Adam, developed the idea of using theme tunes, called *leitmotifs*, for the main characters. Their tunes recur and change subtly throughout the story.

Marie Taglioni was one of the first ballerinas to dance on *pointe*.

Anthony Dowell and Maria Almeida of The Royal Ballet in a real-life scene in *Giselle*.

Romantic ballet today

Few Romantic ballets have survived and later producers have adapted these to suit their audiences. For instance, in the original versions ballerinas were glorified. Today, producers have developed the male roles to make them more equal.

Romantic choreographers

Filippo Taglioni (1779-1871) was the father and teacher of Marie, and choreographer of *La Sylphide* in Paris in 1832.

Auguste Bournonville (1805-1879) recreated *La Sylphide* in 1836 in Copenhagen and choreographed *Napoli* and over 30 other ballets. He is famous for not allowing female dancers to overshadow male ones.

Jules Perrot (1810-1892) created Giselle's dances for the first production in Paris in 1841. Jean Coralli choreographed the rest of *Giselle*.

Romantic dancers

Marie Taglioni (1804-1884) developed the Romantic style and *pointe* work, which allowed her to dance more expressively. Before this, dancers only occasionally went on *pointe* as a kind of trick.

Fanny Elssler (1810-1884) excelled at folk-influenced dances.

Fanny Cerrito (1817-1909) was the most popular ballerina in London.

Carlotta Grisi (1819-1899) was the first Giselle.

Ravenna Tucker and Joseph Cipolla of The Birmingham Royal Ballet in *Giselle*.

Late nineteenth century ballet

Although some people refer to all ballets as "Classical", the term really describes a group of story ballets first produced in Russia around the end of the 19th century. They include *La Bayadère, The Sleeping Beauty, The Nutcracker* and *Swan Lake*. Originally, parts of the stories were just an excuse for a sequence of *divertissements*. Today's producers often improve the stories and characterization.

This typical Classical *pas de deux* pose from *The Sleeping Beauty* is called a fish dive.

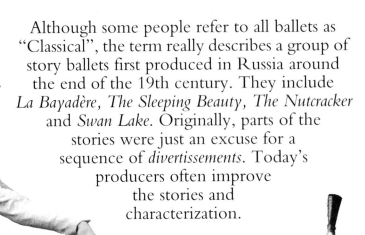

This character is the Bluebird from *The Sleeping Beauty*.

Kevin O'Hare of The Birmingham Royal Ballet.

New developments

By the end of the Romantic period, dancers had developed new skills, such as the ability to dance on *pointe* and look weightless. Ballet teachers now developed new training methods to produce strong dancers with great technical ability. Choreographers began to design ballets primarily to show off the dancers' new skills. Story, costume, design and music often took second place.

By the late 19th century, *pointe* shoes were a standard part of female costume.

Miyako Yoshida of The Birmingham Royal Ballet in *Don Quixote*.

Music for Classical ballet

Classical ballet music was usually composed to order and was often second-rate. It contributed little to the atmosphere, but gave the choreographer the required rhythms and phrase lengths to set his steps to. The exception to this was the music composed by Tchaikovsky. He produced great musical scores for *The Nutcracker, The Sleeping Beauty* and *Swan Lake*. His music is one of the reasons why these great Classical ballets have survived and are still enjoyed by audiences today.

This set for the English National Ballet's production of *The Sleeping Beauty* shows how elaborate the designs for Classical ballet often are.

José Manuel Carreño of The Royal Ballet.

Classical ballet structure

The standard structure consists of three or four acts. Most acts begin with an entrance parade.

Each act is usually built around a *pas de deux* and solos for the leading male and female.

An act also usually includes *corps de ballet* dances as well as smaller group dances.

Character dances are based on national dances and provide a contrast with the balletic style.

Dance style

See if you can spot these features of technique when watching a Classical ballet.

* An erect body, even during difficult jumps and high leg lifts.

* Rapid, precise use of the legs and feet, without affecting the torso.

* Legs raised very high.

* Arms often held in one of the main positions (see page 36).

* Head and eyes usually directed at the audience, as if the dancers are showing themselves off.

* Fast, multiple *pirouettes* and turning steps, particularly at the end of solos.

Classical ballet today

Today, Classical ballets often have the largest budgets. For instance, in a recent production of *The Sleeping Beauty* by The Birmingham Royal Ballet, over fifty wigs and a hundred and fifty hand-sewn costumes were made for a cast of eighty dancers. Classical ballets are spectacular to watch, both in choreography and design.

Famous choreographers

Jules Perrot (1810–1892) was the first of a succession of French choreographers to work with the Imperial Russian Ballet in St. Petersburg.

Arthur St. Léon (1821–1870), Perrot's successor, created *Coppélia* in Paris.

Marius Petipa (1818–1910) created *The Sleeping Beauty, Swan Lake, Raymonda, La Bayadère* and *Don Quixote* among others. He was a Frenchman who became Ballet Master of the Imperial Russian Ballet in 1862 until his death. His career spanned the entire Classical era, which peaked due to his spectacular works

Lev Ivanov (1834–1901), Petipa's assistant, is famous for *The Nutcracker* and the "white acts" (Acts 2 and 4) in *Swan Lake*. These were expressive, rather than just technical displays.

Internet links For links to websites with more information on these famous choreographers, go to **www.usborne-quicklinks.com**

This character is Princess Florine from *The Sleeping Beauty*.

Karen Donovan of The Birmingham Royal Ballet.

In a Classical *pas de deux*, the man presents the woman without drawing attention to himself.

These dancers are wearing typical Classical costumes. The *tutu* was the main costume innovation of the time.

Darcey Bussell and Zoltan Solymosi of The Royal Ballet in *Swan Lake*.

Early twentieth century ballet

The *corps de ballet* of The Birmingham Royal Ballet performing *Choreartium*.

Like many artistic developments, the style of early 20th century ballet was a reaction against that of the previous century. Ballets were no longer based on a sequence of displays of amazing technique. Creating a convincing atmosphere using dance, music and design in equal parts was now the objective. Below, you can see how some of the conventions of Classical ballet were broken.

Tamara Karsavina and Vaslav Nijinsky of the Ballets Russes in *Le Spectre de la Rose*.

Agents of change

At the turn of the century, the Russian choreographer Mikhail Fokine felt that ballet had become mere gymnastics. He also felt that the design and music for a ballet should play a bigger part, working with the choreography. He broke away from the formal structure of Classical ballet and made one-act ballets which used male dancers equally with ballerinas.

Fokine choreographed for Sergei Diaghilev, whose brilliance lay in directing and bringing together the genius of others, whether they were dancers, choreographers, composers or designers. He was able to combine dance, music and design in one artistic whole.

Peter Schaufuss of the London Festival Ballet.

Between 1909 and 1929, Diaghilev's company, the Ballets Russes, toured Europe and America. It revitalized ballet and attracted new talent wherever it went. Some audiences were shocked by the new things that they saw, but others were delighted.

Internet link
For a link to a website with more information about Diaghilev and the Ballets Russes, go to **www.usborne-quicklinks.com**

A programme for the Ballets Russes.

RUSSIAN BALLET

ROYAL OPERA COVENT GARDEN · SEASON 1912 ·

SIXPENCE NET

LONDON·JOHN LONG L^{TD}

This costume was worn by Nijinsky, the first Petrushka. The dancer's body is pathetically bent and limp, and his feet are turned in. This pose would not occur in an earlier ballet.

Famous choreographers

Mikhail Fokine (1880-1942) was Diaghilev's first choreographer. His works include *The Firebird*.

Vaslav Nijinsky (1890-1950) was a legendary dancer who choreographed *Rite of Spring*, *L'Apres-midi d'un Faune* and *Jeux*.

Bronislava Nijinska (1891-1972) choreographed ballets for Diaghilev, such as *Les Noces* and *Les Biches*.

Leonide Massine (1895-1979) also worked for Diaghilev. His ballet *Choreartium* was one of the first abstract works.

George Balanchine (1904-1983) joined Diaghilev as a young dancer. His greatest works of this period were *Apollo* and *The Prodigal Son*.

Frederick Ashton (1904-1988) began choreographing for young British companies. Early theme ballets inlcude *Façade*.

This costume was designed by Bakst in 1921 for the Wicked Fairy's pageboy in *The Sleeping Princess*.

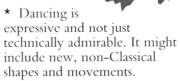

The picture above shows the backcloth designed by Bakst for *The Firebird*.

Design for the ballet

Diaghilev used famous designers such as Bakst, Benois and Picasso to design his ballets. Backcloths, scenery and costume were often great works of art in themselves and no longer just trivial decoration.

The quality of music also became more important. Instead of the choreographer dictating a format to the composer, the two began to work together. Some choreographers were inspired by existing music. Fokine used pieces by Chopin to create a ballet based on sylphs (fairylike spirits) in the moonlight. It became the first theme ballet – *Les Sylphides*.

Dance style

In an early 20th century ballet, such as *The Firebird*, you might be able to notice some of the following aspects of technique which differ from the much more formal style of Classical ballet.

★ Dancing is expressive and not just technically admirable. It might include new, non-Classical shapes and movements.

★ The *corps de ballet* may not all move as one. The patterns they make may be asymmetrical.

★ More expressive, dramatic choreography means that conventional mime gestures may not be needed to tell the story.

The Firebird, a mythical creature, is one of the few characters to wear a *tutu* and *pointe* shoes in a ballet of this period.

Fiona Chadwick of The Royal Ballet.

Internet link For a link to a website about *The Firebird*, go to **www.usborne-quicklinks.com**

Late twentieth century ballet

Today's choreographers have all the past styles to draw upon for inspiration, as well as the freedom to present movement in new ways. They may borrow from other dance styles, such as tap, jazz, ballroom and contemporary dance, as well as national dance styles. Relationships between men and women are less purely romantic and more realistically shown than before.

These zebra characters appear in David Bintley's *Still Life at the Penguin Café.*

Miyako Yoshida and Kevin O'Hare in MacMillan's *Romeo and Juliet.*

Costume and scenery

Today, there are no strict conventions on design. The main limitations are the budget, and the type of space in which the ballet will be performed. As long as the dancers can move easily, the choreographer and designer can dress them in whatever suits the theme of the ballet.

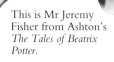

This is Mr Jeremy Fisher from Ashton's *The Tales of Beatrix Potter.*

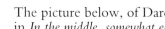

William Trevitt of The Royal Ballet.

Choreographic style

The picture below, of Darcey Bussell in *In the middle, somewhat elevated* (William Forsythe, 1988) shows the freedom that has developed in choreography. Her arms are not in a standard position (see page 36) and her palms are turned away like a jazz dancer's. Instead of looking effortless, her body seems more athletic.

Female dancers still usually wear *pointe* shoes although the rest of the costume might be unconventional.

Alessandra Ferri of the American Ballet Theater.

Inspiration for ballet

A ballet can be about anything. Some examples of themes include the Holocaust (Kenneth MacMillan's *Valley of Shadows*), concern for the environment (David Bintley's *Still Life at the Penguin Café*), the death of a friend (Kenneth MacMillan's *Requiem*, after the death of John Cranko) or a gentle love story (Frederick Ashton's *La Fille Mal Gardée*).

Choreographers devise new lifts and original positions for dramatic effect.

Darcey Bussell and Jonathan Cope of The Royal Ballet.

Famous choreographers

Ninette de Valois (1898-2001) was a British dancer who performed with Diaghilev's Ballets Russes. She later founded the British companies which became The Royal Ballet and The Birmingham Royal Ballet, and also the Royal Ballet School. As well as choreographing her own work, she encouraged other younger choreographers, such as Frederick Ashton and Kenneth MacMillan.

Frederick Ashton (1904-1988) became choreographer for what later became The Royal Ballet in 1935. He created many ballets which were considered to have a very English style. His works from this period include *Cinderella, The Two Pigeons, La Fille Mal Gardée* and *A Month in the Country.*

Sandra Madgwick of The Birmingham Royal Ballet in *La Fille Mal Gardée.*

George Balanchine (1904-1983) founded what became the New York City Ballet, where he perfected the abstract ballet. These include *Concerto Barocco, Theme and Variations, Divertimento, Piano Concerto No. 2, Agon* and *Symphony in C.* Theme ballets include *The Four Temperaments.*

Glen Tetley (born 1926) became Director of the Stuttgart Ballet in 1973. He was the first to attempt to blend modern dance and ballet. His works include *Voluntaries* (1973).

John Cranko (1927-1973) was a South African dancer who joined de Valois' company in 1946. He became director of the Stuttgart Ballet in 1961. His theme ballets include *Card Game* and his story ballets include *Pineapple Poll* and *Onegin.*

Kenneth MacMillan (1929-1992) choreographed for The Royal Ballet, and from 1966-1969 for the *Deutsche Oper* in Berlin. He created a number of short story ballets, such as *Winter Dreams.* His long story ballets include *Romeo and Juliet* and *Manon.* His abstract ballets include *Concerto* and *Danses Concertantes.* His theme ballets include *Elite Syncopations* and *Solitaire.*

Viviana Durante and William Trevitt of The Royal Ballet as Titania and Oberon in Frederick Ashton's *The Dream.* This ballet is based on Shakespeare's *A Midsummer Night's Dream.*

Ballet shoes

There are many different types of shoes used for ballet; they all have special features. Most ballet roles for female dancers require *pointe* shoes. The *pointe* shoe is supposed to make the foot look like a smooth extension of the leg. A ballet company normally provides a dancer with ten pairs of *pointe* shoes a month. A principal dancer, though, is usually allowed twelve.

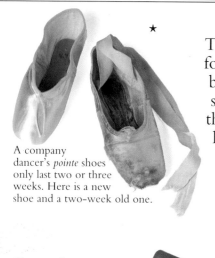

A company dancer's *pointe* shoes only last two or three weeks. Here is a new shoe and a two-week old one.

Each dancer in a company has a pigeon hole in which his or her shoes are kept.

Internet link
For a link to a website with lots more information about *pointe* shoes, go to **www.usborne-quicklinks.com**

Character boots are usually worn for national dances. They are sturdy, with a proper sole and heel. The design varies.

Men and boys wear canvas or leather flat shoes, or "flats". These have thin soles made of leather or suede which bend to show the arch of the foot.

Women usually wear broken down *pointe* shoes for class. Some, though, find leather flats, like these, more comfortable.

Men's character shoes are worn in some roles. They are low-heeled lace-ups. Some have an elasticated buckle on the front.

Girls usually wear satin flat shoes.

Women's character shoes are heeled leather shoes with a strap. They are worn in some roles.

Pointe shoes have a layer of satin on the outside and canvas on the inside. Between these layers, around the dancer's toes, is a stiffened layer of glue or paste, which forms the hard point. This provides support for the dancer's foot, as do the thicker soles. When the toes of the shoes become soft, they can be rehardened with shellac varnish.

Ballet boots are like flat shoes with leather socks attached. They have the flexibility of a flat shoe but boots are more suited to certain costumes.

Jazz shoes are made of soft leather. They are almost as flexible as flat ballet shoes and so are easy to dance in. They come in lots of different shades and go well with some costumes, especially more modern ones.

Sewing on ribbons and elastics

Ballet shoemakers let you decide how to fix the shoes onto your feet. Traditionally, dancers sew their own ribbons on. Here is one method that they use.

You need four ribbons about 2.5cm (1in) wide and 50cm (1½ft) long. Fold the heel so that it lies flat along the sole.

Position the ribbons on the insides of the shoe, just in front of the folds on either side, as shown in the picture above.

Sew the ribbon to the inside canvas rather than through to the outer fabric. Avoid the drawstring on the edge of the shoe.

For elastics, you need a piece for each shoe about 1cm (½in) wide and 12cm (5in) long. Position them by the folds, as for ribbons.

Buying pointe shoes

You should only buy *pointe* shoes when your teacher thinks you are ready to go on *pointe*. Then, you need to find a specialist shop, where the assistant is qualified to fit them correctly. The shoes must fit snugly so they don't move around on your feet. The sole needs to be the right thickness for you. If it is too thick, your foot cannot arch properly. If it is too thin, it will not support your foot.

Break *pointe* shoes in by walking in them at home, until they soften and shape to your feet. Some dancers bang their shoes on concrete to soften them and make them quieter.

Satin *pointe* shoes can be dyed in order to match different costumes.

Tying the ribbons

Don't tie ribbons too tightly or they will restrict your ankle. If they are too loose, though, your shoes might slip.

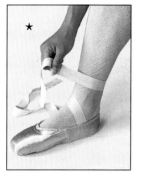

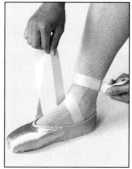

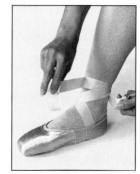

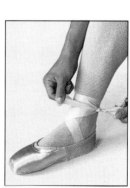

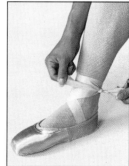

Put your foot flat on the floor. Take the inside ribbon and pass it over your foot and around the back of your ankle to the front.

Pass this ribbon around the back of your ankle again, and bring it to the inside. Take hold of the outer ribbon.

Pass the outer ribbon over your foot and around the back of your ankle. Bring it over your foot and to the inside of your ankle.

Knot the ribbons firmly just above the inside of your ankle in a double knot. Then tuck the loose ends in neatly.

Most dancers use nylon ribbon as satin is too slippery and shiny.

17

Costume

Costumes do more than just look interesting or attractive. They can give clues to the character, or the setting of the ballet. They must allow free and energetic movement, without coming apart. For a new ballet, costumes are made to fit individual dancers. When a ballet is restaged, expensive costumes may be altered for the new cast, rather than new ones being made.

In Romantic ballets, female dancers' hair is usually held in a low bun.

Internet links
For links to websites where you can find out more about costumes, go to **www.usborne-quicklinks.com**

This sleeveless Romantic costume shows the arms clearly.

Romantic costume

By the Romantic period in the early 19th century, ballet skirts had become lighter and shorter. This meant the dancer could jump higher and the audience could see the movements of her calves and feet clearly.

The skirt is made of gauzy, slightly transparent layers so that it floats as the dancer moves.

Alessandra Ferri of the American Ballet Theatre.

This costume design of 1681 shows that before the Romantic period, ballet costumes were based on heavy court fashions.

The standard Romantic or Classical costume for men is tights with a jacket or shirt.

The Classical *tutu* is tight around the waist and hips, making it easier for the male dancer to hold and lift the female.

★ The headdress must be firmly pinned on to withstand fast head movements.

Classical costume

In the Classical era, dancers' skirts were shortened further to show off their intricate legwork. The costume called the *tutu* developed. A *tutu* like the one on the left, with a stiff bodice and lots of material in the skirt, feels less comfortable than the usual practice clothes. Dancers often rehearse in old costumes to get used to the feel.

★

Hooks and eyes are normally used to fasten costumes because they are unlikely to come undone during an energetic dance.

The *tutu* is one complete garment. It shows off the whole line of the leg, so the audience can see the full extent of the ballerina's movements.

Lee Fisher and Rachel Peppin of The Birmingham Royal Ballet.

Twentieth century costume

Twentieth century costumes range from simple leotards to elaborate and authentic period clothes, depending on the nature of the ballet. For instance, the costume on the right was designed by Leon Bakst for *Oriental Impressions*. Consequently, it has a far eastern look to suit its theme. It was worn by Anna Pavlova dancing in London in 1913.

The costume is decorated with jewels and flimsy scarves to give it a rich, mysterious appearance.

The dancer wears oriental-style slippers on her feet.

Vicki Attard as Red Riding Hood in the Australian Ballet's production of *The Sleeping Beauty*.

Roland Price, Petter Jacobsson and Joseph Cipolla of The Birmingham Royal Ballet.

The picture above shows Red Riding Hood in *The Sleeping Beauty*. The costume suggests a previous century, as the story is set firmly in the past. The dancers on the right, however, are wearing thick, stretchy tights, which look very bright and modern. Stretchy fabrics are easy to dance in, but show the dancer's every muscle and any physical imperfections.

A costume designer has to understand how the appearance of fabrics alters under stage lighting. Dull shades can be brought to life and bright ones can change their tone.

Male costumes

The jackets in many male costumes are in two parts. The sleeves are sewn onto a strong, inner bodice. An outer vest-like, sleeveless part of the jacket is worn on top.

The two parts allow the dancer greater flexibility of movement around the shoulders, which is important for lifting the ballerina. However, the garment looks like a single piece to the audience.

The jacket on the right is part of the costume of Prince Florimund in *The Sleeping Beauty*. You can see the two separate parts.

The sleeves are attached to an inner bodice.

Separate, outer jacket.

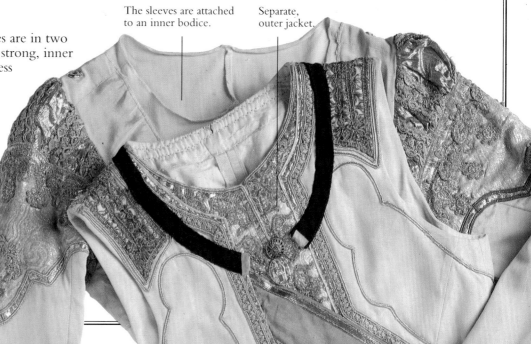

Making a ballet

Before dancers can perform, the dance steps have to be created. The person who does this is called a choreographer. A choreographer's main job is to invent and arrange combinations of steps for ballets, musicals, or any kind of dance performance. Ballet companies often employ their own choreographer to create new ballets and to recreate old ones.

Companies commission photographs to advertise new ballets, such as this one for *Sylvia* by The Birmingham Royal Ballet.

Internet link For a link to a website where you can read a diary by choreographer Christopher Hampson, go to **www.usborne-quicklinks.com**

All dance sequences, such as this one from the film *Strictly Ballroom*, need to be choreographed carefully.

A new ballet

When a company wants to present a new ballet, it asks a choreographer to create a new work and sets a date when it will be performed to the public. The choreographer then decides on a story or a theme. Inspiration can come from anywhere – from an existing story, or from a simple image, such as working machinery.

Gloria, performed here by The Royal Ballet, is a theme ballet inspired by the First World War.

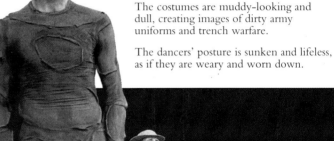

The dancers wear hats designed to resemble army helmets.

The costumes are muddy-looking and dull, creating images of dirty army uniforms and trench warfare.

The dancers' posture is sunken and lifeless, as if they are weary and worn down.

Writing music

Some ballets are set to music which has already been composed. In this case, the choreographer begins by putting a story to it. However, it may not be possible to change existing music to suit the choreographer's ideas.

Another option is to commission music to suit the story or theme. The composer might begin to write by working from a scenario (an outline of how the story will appear on stage) written by the choreographer. The two may work closely together right from the beginning, shaping their ideas as they go along.

The choreographer David Bintley watches rehearsals of *Sylvia*.

Thinking up steps

Different choreographers have different ways of working. Before they begin to rehearse the ballet with the dancers, some already have many of the steps in mind. Others may only have an idea of where the characters come in and where the storyline changes with the music. Choreographers research the subject of the ballet carefully in order to create the right look or style of movement.

Assistant Director of The Birmingham Royal Ballet, Desmond Kelly, rehearses Joseph Cipolla in *Romeo and Juliet*.

Working with the dancers

Six to ten weeks before the ballet is due to be performed, the choreographer goes into the studio to work with the dancers. As they rehearse, the dancers contribute their own ideas. A choreographer can be inspired by the dancers and the amazing things they are capable of. Together they try out different steps, until they find the right ones.

Many steps may be tried out in a short space of time. It can be difficult for everyone to remember what they did and which steps were agreed on. To help, a notator works in the studio and writes down all the steps as they happen. The finest details are recorded accurately.

Internet link
For a link to a website where you can read a rehearsal diary by choreographer Leigh Witchel, go to
www.usborne-quicklinks.com

David Bintley rehearses Miyako Yoshida and Kevin O'Hare of The Birmingham Royal Ballet for *Sylvia*.

Creating new roles

Although a particular dancer may have been chosen for a certain role right from the beginning, a choreographer has to bear in mind that many other dancers may dance that role. For instance, if acrobatic steps are created for a dancer who is also a gymnast, other dancers may not be able to reproduce those steps in the future.

Every dancer has their own particular gifts. It is up to the choreographer to bring out those gifts and perhaps create something for them that they have never done before. Some dancers, however, suit particular roles. For instance, some are very good technicians, but they may not be able to do a difficult dramatic role. So, those dancers who are also good actors often dance the character roles, while those who are excellent technicians may dance the principal roles.

A dramatic role, such as that of Tybalt in *Romeo and Juliet* shown on the right, may be danced by a character artist.

Peter Ottevanger of The Birmingham Royal Ballet.

The final touches

As the first night approaches, rehearsals continue. If the ballet is not right, it is reworked until it improves. It cannot be cancelled as tickets will have been sold and all the preparations will have been made. Changes can be made at the very last minute, or even during a run of performances. A lot of hard work is put in before everyone is happy.

The choreographer Robert Cohan works with the Scottish Ballet in a dress rehearsal of *A Midsummer Night's Dream*.

Staging a ballet

Once a new ballet has been commissioned from a choreographer, or a company has decided to bring an old ballet back to the stage, it has to prepare for the stage performances. Many different people work for a ballet company and a lot of organization is required to make sure everything is ready for the opening night.

Many people from engineers to artists are involved in staging a ballet.

Stage designs, such as this front cloth from *Romeo and Juliet*, bring atmosphere to the ballet.

Internet link
For links to websites with details on staging ballets, go to
www.usborne-quicklinks.com

Design ideas

A choreographer is often not only the inventor of the dance steps, but is also the author of the ballet's story and the director in control of it. For these reasons, the choreographer often has a big influence over the design.

The choreographer may have a good idea of what scenery, costume or lighting will match the story or music. The choreographer discusses these ideas with the designer, who brings them to life.

For instance, in the ballet *Street*, lighting is important. The theme is a day in a hot climate and the lighting conveys different moods. It starts in the cool early morning, progresses through the heat of noon and a restless evening, to end in a party atmosphere at night.

This scene from *Street*, danced by Jessica Clarke and Evan Williams of The Birmingham Royal Ballet, is lit in cool purple to signify the dawn.

This scene, danced by Monica Zamora and Joseph Cipolla, is lit in warm orange to convey the atmosphere of early evening.

This scenery from *Romeo and Juliet* was inspired by the architecture of Italy in the Middle Ages, where the story is set.

The ballet develops

While the scenario is being thought out and the music is taking shape, the set design develops. For instance, the position of a door on stage may have a direct influence over the music. It may take ten seconds for a dancer to reach the door, or it may take half a minute, so the music has to match accordingly.

Tailors and seamstresses make costumes in the workrooms.

In the same way, the dance steps have a direct influence over the set design. For instance, there may be a scene where a dancer flies through a window, which means that the window must be big enough for her to get through safely.

The choreographer and the designers also have to take into account the schedules of the rest of the company. They have to think ahead and plan their work. For instance, the costumes for a ballet may have to be made six months before the choreography is completed, because that is when the workrooms are free.

Once it has been designed, builders make the set and artists paint it. This set is from Robert Cohan's *A Midsummer Night's Dream*.

Engineers arrange the lighting to achieve the effects that the director wants.

Restaging ballets

As well as commissioning new ballets, companies often restage old ones. Ballets from the 20th century are rarely changed – they are usually restaged as they were done originally. However, older ones are often recreated by inventing new choreography or designing new scenery and costumes in order to inject new life into them.

This is done because a modern audience would probably not appreciate an old ballet in its original version. Today, the dancers are technically better and are more impressive. Modern costumes and scenery are also more stunning.

Ballets such as *Swan Lake*, however, are traditional and audiences expect to see them presented in a traditional way. Many of the steps are very good as they are, so a choreographer would be unlikely to change the major parts. However, the idea is to bring something exciting to the audience – whether the ballet is traditional or absolutely brand new.

A member of the *corps de ballet* in *Swan Lake*, produced by The Royal Ballet in 1993.

A member of the *corps de ballet* in *Swan Lake*, produced in 1934 for the Vic-Wells Ballet.

Performing on stage

Dancing in costume, to a full orchestra and in front of an audience, is not the same as rehearsing in a familiar studio. The costume might be heavy and restricting, the orchestra might play at slightly different speeds to those the dancer is used to, and the stage might be harder than the studio floor. All these things put pressure on dancers and push them to put on their best performance.

Dancers of the Bolshoi Ballet taking a curtain call.

Countdown to the performance

4:30 pm *Have a snack and a drink.*

5:00 pm *Choose and clean pointe shoes.*

5:30 pm *Do makeup and hair, fixing headdress or wig. Put on practice clothes.*

6:30 pm *Warm up at barres on the stage.*

6:55 pm *The stage manager calls the "half" over the tannoy system. This tells the dancers there is half an hour before everything must be ready for the performance. All understudies must be in the theatre by now. Dancers begin to put on shoes and costumes, with warm clothes over the top.*

7:10 pm *The stage manager calls the "quarter": 15 minutes left. Dancers check that their own props are in position.*

7:20 pm *The stage manager calls the "five": five minutes left. Any costumes for quick changes are set up in the wings by the wardrobe staff.*

7:25 pm *Those dancers who are on stage at the start of the performance, called "beginners", must come down to the stage.*

7:29 pm *The stage manager clears the stage and calls "stand-by". Dancers in the wings remove warm clothes.*

7:30 pm *When the house lights have dimmed, the conductor enters the orchestra pit. The audience applauds and the overture begins. At the right moment, the stage manager gives the cue to pull the curtain up.*

Dancers of The Royal Ballet warming up at a portable *barre* before a performance.

Understudying

If a dancer is injured or unwell, or is hurt during the show, an understudy needs to take over the role. However, an understudy does not have to stay in the theatre after the performance has begun, unless the person they are understudying is not feeling perfectly well. If the understudy has gone, a different dancer might have to take over. This is usually someone who knows the ballet and its style well, so that if necessary they can improvise, or follow whispered instructions from other members of the cast, without the audience noticing.

If anything goes wrong...

If a dancer falls, or performs a step badly, he or she must carry on as if nothing has happened. The audience may not even notice. A strong finish can make up for earlier weaknesses in the performance.

If the dancer is hurt, the stage manager has an ice pack which can reduce pain and swelling. A hormone called adrenalin also helps to kill pain so the dancer might still be able to finish the show.

Backstage, dancers get ready in dressing rooms.

Makeup

Powder

Pansticks

Dancers wear makeup to exaggerate their features so that the audience can see their faces and expressions clearly. Makeup also gives brightness and shape to the face which can look pale and flat under strong stage lighting. Dancers use makeup to alter their features if they need to portray a character different to their own. Male makeup is usually less vivid than female makeup.

Greasepaint sticks

Pancake can be used as foundation.

False eyelashes

★

Makeup brushes

Mascara

Lipsticks

Rouge

Eye shadows

Eye pencils

Cleanser

Pads for makeup removal.

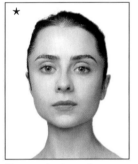
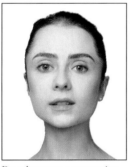

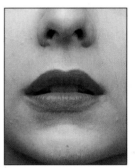

A female dancer's makeup

Female dancers usually allow about an hour to do their makeup and hair before a performance.

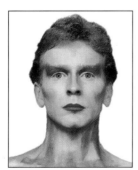

Greasepaint is used as foundation, with panstick for shadows and highlights.

Powder stops greasepaint from smudging or looking shiny under the hot, bright stage lights.

Eyeliner and eye shadow are applied and false eyelashes glued on to darken the eyes.

Rouge or blusher and lipstick are applied last of all, to complete the dancer's makeup.

She can now do her hair and put on her headdress.

The makeup for Satan

These pictures show how Michael O'Hare of The Birmingham Royal Ballet transforms himself into Satan, from Ninette de Valois' *Job*.

The body is made up at the same time.

A layer of greasepaint and panstick provides the base makeup and adds shape to the face.

Green panstick gives an unearthly appearance. Red details are added to the lips, eyes and nose.

Black lines are added to exaggerate the features and make the face look dramatic.

Belonging to a company

Many ballet companies have ballet schools attached to them, and the best graduates from the school may be invited to join the company. Other new members may join after an audition. A company without a school attached to it will advertise for dancers and hold auditions. A dancer's contract with a company comes up for renewal each year, so the positions are not particularly secure.

The *corps de ballet* of The Birmingham Royal Ballet in *Les Sylphides.*

Tutus hang upside down for storage to protect the outer layers of the bodice and skirt.

Daily routine

The company's routine depends on whether it is at home or on tour, rehearsing or performing. There is always a daily class, though. All classes have the same basic structure.

Hair is worn away from the neck and face, so that the line made by the head and neck can be seen.

These dancers are rehearsing an *attitude.*

★

The class is an important part of the day. During rehearsal weeks, the goal is to develop strength, stamina, suppleness and dance quality. During a run of performances, it is less strenuous because the dancers need to stay fresh.

Leg warmers keep muscles and joints warm.

Dancers in class wear lightweight, stretchy clothes, which are often very old, so they are as comfortable as possible.

Rehearsals

Rehearsals ("calls") take up the rest of the day until two hours before an evening performance. If there is no performance, rehearsals may continue into the evening. Not every dancer is needed for every call. If a dancer is performing in the evening, they are allowed to take part in no more than three hours' rehearsal. Meals, rests, shoe preparation and costume fittings all need to be fitted into the day. If dancers have any injuries, they may also have to find time to see a physiotherapist.

Internet links
For links to websites where you can find even more links to ballet companies around the world, and to read about a day in the life of a ballet dancer, go to **www.usborne-quicklinks.com**

The hierarchy in a ballet company

In the past, the hierarchy in a company was rigid and promotion took years. Today, directors and choreographers are quick to spot new talent and may give dancers principal opportunities in their first years with a company.

Corps de ballet (artists) belong to the lowest rank. There are usually more women than men in this rank because of the frequent use of large female groups in ballets. Many dancers remain in the *corps de ballet* for their whole careers.

Coryphées (first artists or junior soloists) are promising members of the *corps de ballet* who have been promoted to this rank and given solo parts. However they will probably also continue to dance with the *corps de ballet*.

Soloists, as well as dancing solos, may as understudies learn principal roles and occasionally perform them. Some companies have a **senior soloist**, or **first soloist**, rank. Senior soloists probably perform several principal roles.

Principals and **senior principals** are the company's star performers and often appear in leading roles. There are as many men as women in this rank. Principal dancers may also appear with different companies as guest artists from time to time.

Character artists are respected senior members of the company who specialize in dramatic roles which require a lot of acting, as well as dancing, ability. Roles such as the Nurse in *Romeo and Juliet* may be performed by a character artist.

This picture shows the cast of the Scottish Ballet performing in *The Nutcracker*. The soloists kneel around the principals in the middle, while the *corps de ballet* are at the back.

On tour

Companies go on tour both at home and abroad. A foreign tour might last from two weeks to three months. Dancers may have to adapt rapidly to different climates and types of audience. They also have to adjust to stages which vary in size, hardness and rake (that is, how much they slope down to the audience).

If there is no time for a full rehearsal, a "placing call" enables the *corps de ballet* to familiarize themselves with different sizes and shapes of stage. The dancers walk through the moves without dancing them and without music. Principal dancers work alone, checking their entrances and exits and how far steps can travel.

Company staff

Companies have many vital non-dancing members of staff.

Internet link For a link to a website where you can read about a busy wardrobe department, go to **www.usborne-quicklinks.com**

The **director** decides artistic policy – what ballets to perform and who dances which role.

The **ballet master** or **mistress** organizes the rehearsal timetable (call sheet) and takes the dancers through rehearsals.

A **répétiteur** also takes rehearsals.

Dance notators (see pages 28-29) record the steps of new ballets, and teach ballets to a new cast.

Company ballet teachers are in charge of the daily classes.

A **stage manager** makes sure that the performance runs smoothly and organizes the staff in charge of scenery, lighting and props.

Musicians, including the rehearsal pianist and orchestra, provide the music.

Wardrobe staff, including a wig-mistress or master and a shoe specialist, look after the costumes.

Administrative staff organize tour schedules, the dancers' contracts, the accounts and so on.

A **publicity department** deals with the press and produces promotional material, such as posters and photographs.

An **education department** informs people about ballet and dance, which helps to increase audiences.

Recording ballet

Dancers remember all the steps they have to learn with help from written systems called dance notation. There are many different kinds of notation, but two of the most widely used are Benesh notation and Labanotation. People who write down dance steps are called notators. It is very helpful for choreographers to have a notator in the studio while they work, so that newly created step combinations are recorded correctly.

A notator and a pianist check that their scores match.

The notator works with a teacher in the studio.

Benesh notation

Benesh uses a five-line stave, like music, and uses symbols to describe what the dancer's body is doing. The lines of the stave represent the different levels of the body when the dancer is standing up straight, as shown below.

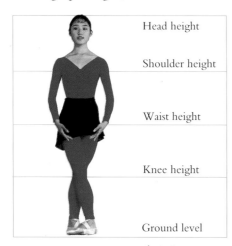

Head height

Shoulder height

Waist height

Knee height

Ground level

The symbols

Symbols representing the hands and feet show how high they are held and if they are in front, behind or level with the body. Curved lines show where movements start and finish. The symbols are written as if the notator is behind the dancer, so that their right and left correspond. Here are some of the main symbols.

Hand or foot level with the body.

Knee or arm bent level with the body.

Hand or foot in front of the body.

Knee or arm bent in front of the body.

Hand or foot behind the body.

Knee or arm bent behind the body.

The five positions of the feet

Here are the five positions of the feet (see page 37) shown in Benesh notation.

First position

Second position

Third position

Fourth position

Fifth position

A sequence in Benesh

Here you can see how Benesh notation corresponds to the movements and positions of a dancer.

Remember that the staves show the position of the dancer from behind, although the photographs have been taken from the front.

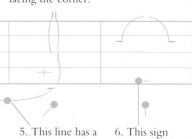

1. She starts with left foot in *tendu* behind, facing the corner.

2. She slides forward into an *arabesque* position.

3. She transfers onto her right foot and faces the front.

4. She jumps to close in fifth position.

5. She jumps back onto her left foot, facing the corner.

6. She ends in fifth position on *pointe*, facing the front.

Internet link
For a link to a website about Benesch, go to **www.usborne-quicklinks.com**

1. This sign shows the direction the dancer is facing.

2. This is a slide line. The "in front" symbol shows it travels forward.

3. This is a step line. It shows a transfer of weight to the other foot.

4. This curved line is a jump line. It reflects the arc of the jump.

5. This line has a "behind" symbol to show that the jump goes back.

6. This sign shows that she is on *pointe*. She stays in one spot.

The dance notator's job

Notators work by noting down what each dancer is doing on each count. They then make a combined record, called a score, showing everyone's movements. On a finished score, each dancer has their steps written on a separate stave. In the picture on the right, a notator helps during a stage rehearsal.

Labanotation

Labanotation uses a vertical three-line stave, as shown on the right, on which the movement symbols are placed. The stave represents the body. The middle line divides it into left and right.

Movements of the legs and feet are written in columns within the three stave lines. Movements of the body, arms and head are written outside the stave in the positions shown.

Internet link
For a link to a website where you can find a more detailed introduction to Labanotation, go to **www.usborne-quicklinks.com**

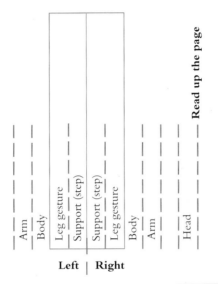

Read up the page

Arm | Body | Leg gesture | Support (step) | Support (step) | Leg gesture | Body | Arm | Head

Left | Right

In previous times, steps were often just remembered by dancers and choreographers. As a result, the choreography of some old ballets has been lost. Today, if a company wants to bring a ballet back to the stage after a few years, all the steps will have been preserved in notation form.

Internet link
For a link to a website where you can read an article comparing notation with video recording, go to **www.usborne-quicklinks.com**

A dance sequence in Labanotation

Here you can see how Labanotation corresponds to the dance seqence shown on page 28. The numbered labels refer to the dancer's positions. The symbols on the stave show the movements of the dancer from behind. Labanotation is read from the bottom up the page. Remember, the length of each symbol shows the time taken to perform it.

The symbols

Symbols are written as if the notator is standing behind the dancer. Each symbol gives four pieces of information – the direction of the movement, its level, its timing and the part of the body which performs it.

Direction
This is shown by the shape of the symbol.

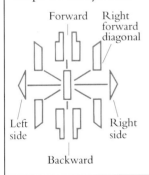

Forward | Right forward diagonal

Left side | Right side

Backward

Level
This is shown by the shading of the symbol.

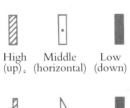

High (up) | Middle (horizontal) | Low (down)

Forward high | Side middle | Backward low

Timing
This is shown by the length of the symbol.

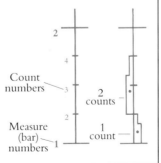

Count numbers

Measure (bar) numbers

2 counts

1 count

The five positions of the feet

Here are the five positions of the feet shown in Labanotation.

First position | Second position | Third position (right foot in front) | Fourth position | Fifth position (right foot in front)

---

6. She faces the front, rising to end on *pointe* in fifth position.

5. This symbol shows that the jump lands backward.

4. She lands with the right foot in front and arms down.

The gap in this column shows she is now in the air.

3. This shows that she now faces the front.

2. These hooks show the forward step slides.

1. This shows the dancer faces downstage left to start.

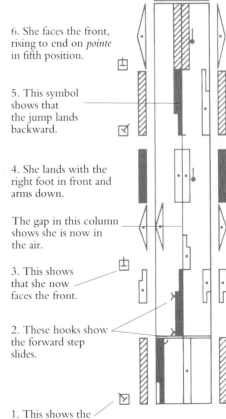

Going to ballet school

For a career as a professional ballet dancer, serious training needs to start by about 11 or 12 for girls and by about 14 for boys. This is because it takes years to develop the correct suppleness, shape and strength in your muscles and bones. Some people go to an ordinary school while studying intensively with a local ballet teacher. Others audition for a full-time ballet school where ballet and academic classes are in one place.

Students at ballet school also learn academic subjects, such as science.

Students train in other styles of dance, such as tap, jazz and national dance.

A dance student's physique

Although dancers can vary in build, there are some physical requirements without which it is difficult to be successful. Some of these are shown here. The students shown on this page are from the National Youth Ballet, which brings talented young dancers together from ballet schools all over Britain. This company offers young dancers the chance to take part in creating and performing ballet in a professional situation.

A dancer needs long, elegant limbs.

A neat, fairly small head can be an advantage.

Strong, supple back

Good turn-out from the hips is essential.

Slender frame

Auditioning for ballet school

Getting a place at ballet school is by audition – a danced test in front of examiners. The examiners look for people with talent, correct physique, sensitivity to music and physical control. The level of previous training is less important than the potential to develop. Pupils are taken by a ballet school at junior or senior level. Juniors are aged 11 and up when they enter the school. Senior students are aged from about 16.

At an audition, junior applicants are asked to do natural movements, such as skips, jumps and gallops, and to improvise movements to music. This shows their natural ability. Seniors do a ballet class at a first audition. Those who are invited back for a final audition might be asked to dance in another style, such as a modern or character dance, or to learn and perform a sequence from the repertory.

Applicants also have a physical examination to check their turn-out and the suppleness and structure of their joints. The shape of a girl's foot is important, for *pointe* work.

Joints should be neither too stiff nor too loose.

The tendons at the backs of the thighs, called hamstrings, should not be too tight.

Straight legs – not bowed or knock-kneed.

Firm muscle tone

Arched feet

Life at a ballet school

Most junior pupils live at ballet school and take normal exams like other children. The day begins with breakfast at about 7:30 am. Pupils then go either to a ballet class or an academic lesson at 8:30 am. Juniors spend about twice as much time in academic lessons as in dance classes.

As well as learning dance, they also have drama, music and choreography lessons. Swimming is encouraged but other sports are carefully monitored as they can cause the wrong muscles or body shape for dancers to develop.

For seniors, the balance of work shifts. They spend far more time at dance classes, with perhaps only an hour or two of academic lessons a day. They usually live in rented rooms outside the school, so they have to do their own shopping, cooking and cleaning.

By now, students are learning *pas de deux* and repertory. Some are offered the chance to understudy the *corps de ballet* with a company. They may even go on tour with it, which serves as a trial apprenticeship.

A major preoccupation for senior students is finding a job. Some audition for a contract with a professional company. Some find jobs in commercial theatre, taking part in musicals. Others may become teachers, notators or choreographers.

Internet links
For links to websites where you can find out about auditions, life at ballet school and read ballet students' diaries, go to **www.usborne-quicklinks.com**

Ballet studios

Ballet schools have large dance studios where the classes take place. Each studio has wall mirrors, a good piano, *barres* and a sprung floor. A sprung floor is constructed so that it gives very slightly when dancers land from a jump. This helps them to avoid jarring their joints. The wooden floor of the studio may be slippery, which can be dangerous. So, students rub the soles of their shoes in a small amount of white powder called rosin, which helps them grip. Professional dancers also use rosin on their shoes to prevent them from slipping and injuring themselves.

School performances

A high point in life at a ballet school is taking part in a school performance. The performances may include ballets from the repertory and ballets specially choreographed for the occasion, as well as dances in other styles – jazz, tap, contemporary and character dance. There may also be a drama production and a chance for students to display their own choreography. Students taking part gain invaluable experience of performing in a theatre in front of an audience and perhaps to a live orchestra, which is enormously helpful to their future careers.

The picture below shows a class of junior girls at the Royal Ballet School exercising at the *barre*.

Some famous schools

Many ballet schools are attached to companies. Below are some examples.

The Royal Ballet School	The Royal Ballet and The Birmingham Royal Ballet
The English National Ballet School	The English National Ballet
The School of American Ballet	The New York City Ballet
The National Ballet School	The National Ballet of Canada
The Royal Danish Ballet School	The Royal Danish Ballet

Internet links
For links to the websites of the schools above, where you can get an idea of ballet school life and the audition procedure, go to **www.usborne-quicklinks.com**

How ballet began

People have always danced. The first dances were probably part of religious ceremonies, but by the time of the Ancient Greeks and Romans, dancing had also become a form of entertainment. In the Middle Ages, the Church in Europe claimed that dancing was sinful, but when the Renaissance arrived around 1450, dancing became popular again. However, it is to the European courts of the 16th and 17th centuries that the beginnings of ballet belong.

Music for early ballet was played on viols, like this one, and horns.

For early ballets, people wore shoes like their ordinary ones, above.

The splendid courts of Europe

In the 16th and 17th centuries, European royalty, especially in Italy and France, made their courts as splendid as possible. They tried to better each other by employing poets, musicians, artists and also dancing masters. Courtiers were trained how to move and behave, and had lessons in fencing and dancing. The style of today's ballet posture follows that of 17th century courtiers. Their spines were held elegantly upright, with turned-out legs to show off shapely calves. Their arms were rounded, with delicately held fingers. Heads were lifted to support heavy wigs and headgear.

Courtiers regularly took part in court entertainments. These spectacles were staged on important occasions, such as royal marriages. They were often based on the myths of Ancient Greece and Rome and included processions, poetic speeches, music and dancing. The dances, which were elegant versions of those performed by country peasants, developed into the first ballets. The whole event, called a *ballet de cour* (court ballet), would be decorated with elaborate scenery and beautiful costumes.

Le Ballet Comique de la Reine is the first known ballet. It was performed in 1581 at the marriage of the Queen of France's sister.

Louis XIV in his costume as the Rising Sun in *Le Ballet de la Nuit*, a *ballet de cour*.

The Sun King

Louis XIV of France, who ruled between 1643 and 1715, took his dancing very seriously. He took part in his first ballet, *Cassandre*, at the age of 12 and trained daily with his dancing master Beauchamp. One of his famous roles was the Rising Sun and this led him to become known as the Sun King. His other famous role was Apollo, the Roman god.

Louis stopped dancing in his thirties and his courtiers lost interest in ballet. However, he had already set up the Académie Royale de Musique et de Danse, which taught properly defined steps. The five positions of the feet (see page 37), which are thought to have been defined by Beauchamp, were now set down by the Académie as the technical basis for ballet style.

Internet links
For links to websites about the origins of ballet, go to **www.usborne-quicklinks.com**

Dancing in operas

Ballet was first seen in the theatre as part of opera, in which dance was included. In 1669, Louis gave permission for an opera house to open in Paris and its first opera *Pomone* included dances by Beauchamp. Although women danced in court ballets, they were not allowed to dance in the theatre until 1681. When they did appear, their long, heavy skirts made their technique more limited than the men's.

By this time professional dancers, instead of courtiers, were dancing in operas. They realized that there was a greater demand for their skills, so they worked harder. As theatrical dancing became popular, it developed more than dancing at social occasions. By 1700, dancers were performing complex and athletic steps.

The first ballet companies

Other European cities soon opened opera houses too. Ballet companies were set up to train people to dance in operas – the first was based at the Paris Opéra in 1713. New steps, such as beaten jumps and *pirouettes* continued to be created in Paris. Female dancers, such as Marie Camargo, began to rival the men and dominate the stage. Marie was a great technician, who became the first woman to perform complex jumps. She is most famous for wearing a short skirt, exposing her ankles, to show off her quick footwork.

The Belgian dancer Marie Camargo is seen here showing her feet and ankles.

Ballet comes into its own

By the mid 18th century, ballet had broken away from opera. It became more expressive as mime and gesture developed to replace words and song. One of the first ballets to do this was *The Loves of Mars and Venus* choreographed by John Weaver in London in 1717.

One of the important choreographers of the time was Jean George Noverre. He insisted on a dramatic plot, rather than many *divertissements* danced to any music. Later choreographers began to make roles based on ordinary people as well as on myths. Ballets were now created to make the audience feel happy or sad, as well as to show them good technique. Ballet was beginning to develop into the Romantic style.

A costume designed by Louis-René Boquet around 1770 for the dancer Gaétan Vestris.

Early choreographers

Jean George Noverre (1727-1810) wrote famously about choreography.

Jean Dauberval (1742-1806) made many comic roles. His best work was an early version of *La Fille Mal Gardée*.

Charles Ludvig Didelot (1767-1836) was the first to "fly" dancers on wires.

Early dancers

Marie Salle (1707-1756) was a moving and expressive performer.

Marie Camargo (1710-1770) was a great technician.

Gaétan Vestris (1729-1808) and his son **Auguste** (1760-1842) were great male dancers. They were both given the title "The God of Dance".

Learning ballet

In ballet class, dancers learn technique and develop their own styles. All classes, however advanced, follow the same basic structure. A class starts with exercises at the *barre,* a handrail which runs along the edges of the studio. The dancers then move into the middle of the studio and work without the support of the *barre.* The class ends with jumps and travelling steps. An advanced class might finish with *pointe* work for females, and extra jump practice for males.

A *développé* at the *barre.*

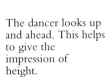

An *attitude* in the centre.

Barre work

Barre work teaches a set of basic movements and also warms up, stretches and strengthens the muscles in the body. The exercises help to prepare the body for more energetic or demanding steps done later in the class. The *barre* acts as a support, helping the dancer to stand and balance correctly. (See pages 38-41 for more about *barre* work, and for illustrations of some *barre* exercises.)

The dancer looks up and ahead. This helps to give the impression of height.

Dancers in class usually jump from one corner of the studio to the diagonally opposite corner, either singly or in pairs.

How classes develop

In the early years of training, the pace of a class is slow and careful, concentrating on simple steps. The training gradually progresses to more complicated movements and sets of steps. This helps students learn how to use their bodies correctly when doing simple movements, so that they avoid damaging themselves when they progress to more difficult movements.

This big jump is called a *grand jeté.*

Centre work

In the centre (see pages 42-45), students repeat some *barre* exercises, but without the *barre,* in order to find their balance. Other centre work exercises involve moving smoothly from one position to another, and turning steps, called *pirouettes.*

Big jumps like this are done near the end of a class, when the body is warm.

Jumps and travelling steps

This part of the class (see pages 46-49) starts with small warm-up jumps, to prepare you for performing higher ones. Some jump steps require fast, intricate footwork. High leaps require power and strength.

Internet links
For links to websites where you can watch video clips of dancers demonstrating steps, consult a ballet dictionary or read a description of an advanced ballet class, go to **www.usborne-quicklinks.com**

Going on pointe

Before she can start to do *pointe* work, a female dancer needs to wait until her feet, ankles and back are strong enough to support her weight correctly. Different people reach this stage at different ages. It depends partly on physical maturity and partly on body structure. A dancer should not go on *pointe* without the approval and supervision of a trained teacher who knows her capabilities.

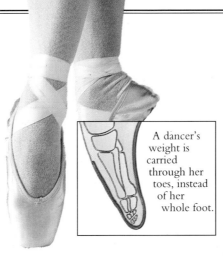

A dancer's weight is carried through her toes, instead of her whole foot.

If you go on *pointe* before your body is strong enough, you might strain your lower back, causing backache. You can strain your knee joints, causing joint disorders in later life. The big toe joint can be pushed out of shape and form a painful bunion. It is important to wear *pointe* shoes that fit you properly. There is advice on buying *pointe* shoes on page 17. Also take advice from your teacher.

Clothing for class

If you are starting a new class, ask the teacher what you should wear. Here are some standard items. Close-fitting clothes enable the teacher to see the shapes made by your body.

Girl's leotard

A hairband keeps hair off your face and neck.

Boy's T-shirt or leotard

Flat ballet shoes

A unitard is an alternative to a leotard and tights, for girls or boys.

Girl's tights

Flat ballet shoes

Boy's white socks

Boy's tights

★

You can wear leg warmers and a sweatshirt until your muscles are warm.

Finding a class

If you want to learn ballet, find a class with a qualified teacher. You don't have to be fit and athletic to learn ballet. You will build strength and suppleness as you go along.

You could ask the teacher whether there will be other students your age in the class and how long they have been dancing. The teacher will probably ask how old you are, whether you have done any dance before and whether you play any sports. These questions will help the teacher start you off in a class at the right level for you.

Dance shows and exams

Taking part in dance shows helps to develop an awareness of where others are on the stage and how you fit into the pattern. Also, it helps you to get used to having an audience.

Ballet exams provide a goal and passing an exam gives you confidence and proof of your progress. If you pass an exam, you may receive a certificate like this one.

Summer schools

Many ballet schools offer dance courses during the summer vacations for children and young people. Classes are held during the day and the courses usually last between one and two weeks.

The courses often concentrate on Classical ballet, but they might also include subjects such as character dancing, jazz, tap, drama, singing, mime, makeup and repertory (learning dances from the ballets). Summer schools are held worldwide in major cities, but places can be scarce as demand for them is high.

Positions of the arms and feet

Most ballet steps begin and end with the arms and feet in one of the positions shown on these pages. There are five numbered arm positions, with three additional arm positions which have French names instead of numbers. There are five main positions of the feet, numbered one to five, with two variations on fourth position.

First position
(en première)

Curve your arms, with fingertips about 5cm (2in) apart and level with your navel.

Demi-bras

This position is in between first position and *bras bas*.

Positions of the arms

In the arm positions, imagine a long, smooth curve from your shoulder to the tip of your middle finger. Avoid sharp angles at your wrists and elbows. Feel that your arms are attached to the middle of your back, not just your shoulders. This helps to keep the shoulders relaxed and your arms supported. Positions can be combined. You can, for instance, have your feet in fifth position and your arms in third.

Second position
(en seconde)

Your palms and the insides of your elbows face the front.

Demi-seconde

This position is half way between second position and *bras bas*.

Third position
(en troisième)

Hold one arm as if it was in second, and the other as if it was in first.

Bras bas

The arms are in the same shape as for first but low, about 5cm (2in) in front of you.

Fourth position
(en quatrième)

Hold one arm as if it was in second, and the other as if it was in fifth (see right).

Fifth position
(en cinquième)

Both arms are curved above and slightly in front of you, about 5cm (2in) apart.

Internet link
For a link to a website where you can find out what's involved when you begin taking ballet lessons, go to **www.usborne-quicklinks.com**

Holding your arm to the side

You should be able to see your fingertips out of the corners of your eyes while looking to the front. If your arms are too far back, this will push your shoulderblades together and your chest out. There should be a gradual slope down from your elbows to your hands.

Positions of the feet

In all these positions, the legs are straight. Your feet are only turned out by the same amount as your knees. Carry your weight on the balls of your feet – your heels touch the floor but do not dig in.

You can put either foot in front in third, fourth and fifth positions. If you are standing with your right hand on the *barre*, you put your left foot in front to start an exercise, and *vice versa*.

Pull your buttock muscles and the muscles at the backs of your thighs together to turn your feet out. Do not turn your feet out more than your knees.

Your toes should be relaxed along the floor – not crunched up.

Doing exercises en croix

When you do an exercise, such as pointing or lifting your foot, you normally do the movement to the front, then to the side, back and side again. This pattern is known as *en croix* (in a cross shape). The diagrams below show an exercise called a *battement tendu* performed *en croix*, starting with the feet in fifth. See pages 40-41 for more exercises performed *en croix*.

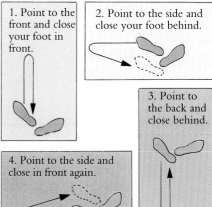

1. Point to the front and close your foot in front.

2. Point to the side and close your foot behind.

3. Point to the back and close behind.

4. Point to the side and close in front again.

Different techniques

Within ballet there are different techniques, such as the Royal Academy of Dancing (RAD) and the Cecchetti Society techniques. The basic movements are the same in all techniques but the combinations of steps vary and some of the arm positions differ. This book follows the RAD technique.

Internet link
For a link to a website where you can find out about Enrico Cecchetti, founder of Cecchetti ballet, go to **www.usborne-quicklinks.com**

Taking part in a class

Here are some guidelines for how to get the best out of your ballet classes, whatever your level of training.

★ Arrive on time. If you are late, you might distract other students, and miss warm-up exercises.

★ Attend regularly so you can make progress and build up your fitness.

★ Listen to instructions and concentrate on what you can get out of each exercise.

★ Don't be distracted by other people in the class.

★

First position *(en première)*
Put your heels together and turn out your feet and legs.

★

Open fourth *(en quatrième ouverte)*
Place one foot directly forward from first position by about 30cm (1ft).

★
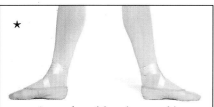
Second position *(en seconde)*
Place your feet apart by about one and a half times your foot's length.

★

Crossed fourth *(en quatrième croisée)*
Place one foot directly forward from fifth position (see below).

★
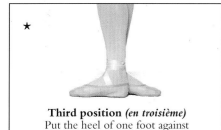
Third position *(en troisième)*
Put the heel of one foot against the middle of your other foot.

★

Fifth position *(en cinquième)*
Put the heel of one foot against the big toe joint of your other foot.

Basic steps at the *barre*

Barre exercises aim to increase the flow of blood to your muscles so that they receive more oxygen and can work harder. The *barre* helps you to support yourself so that you can concentrate on moving and holding different parts of your body in the proper relationship to each other. You do *barre* exercises facing one way and then facing the other, to work both sides of your body equally.

A dancer warming up at the *barre*.

To work on *barre* exercises at home, use the back of a chair.

Keep your head up and your chin level – not sticking out.

Relax your shoulders to help lengthen your neck.

Relax your fingers and thumb on top of the *barre*, slightly in front of you.

When you point your foot to the side, your toes should be level with the toes of the other leg. There should be no weight on your pointed foot.

Use your stomach muscles to keep your stomach supported and flat.

Your bottom should be down and not sticking out.

★

The leg nearest the *barre* is called your supporting leg. The other leg is called your working leg. This is the leg you exercise.

Pointing your foot

When you point your foot, there should be a straight line from your hip down through your knee, your ankle and out through your middle toe, as shown in the picture on the left. Don't clench your toes or let your foot curl in, or "sickle".

Placement

The correct positioning of one part of your body in relation to another is called placing or placement. To help your placement, imagine a straight line running from the top of your head through the middle of your body and ending between your feet. Imagine another line across your hips, keeping them level. Try to keep these lines steady as you exercise.

Standing at the barre

The *barre* should be high enough so that when you rest your hand on it, your torso and shoulders remain level. Many studios have two *barres* at different heights so you can choose which is best for you. Stand at a distance from the *barre* that allows your upper body to stay undistorted. Your elbow should not be in the way and cause your body to twist.

Pliés

Pliés stretch your leg muscles and improve your turn-out. There are two types of *pliés: demi-pliés* (half knee bends) and *grands pliés* (full knee bends). You can do *pliés* in all five positions of the feet (see pages 37). There are three examples below. The arms move smoothly through the positions shown in the pictures. Try to retain a lifted appearance as you bend your knees. It helps to imagine that you are staying the same height and that your spine is lengthening down to the ground.

Keep your knees pointing out over your toes.

Throughout a *plié*, keep your weight evenly over both feet.

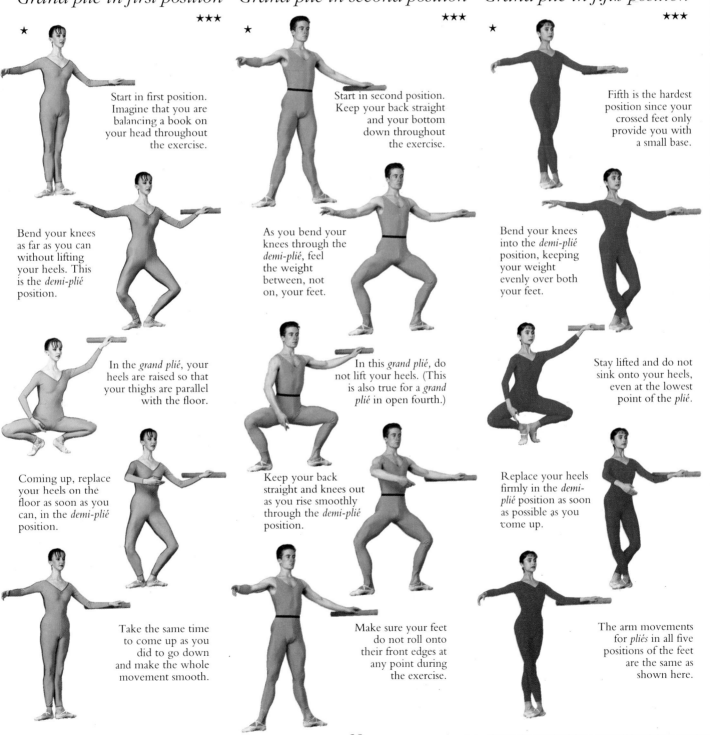

Grand plié in first position ★★★

★ Start in first position. Imagine that you are balancing a book on your head throughout the exercise.

Bend your knees as far as you can without lifting your heels. This is the *demi-plié* position.

In the *grand plié*, your heels are raised so that your thighs are parallel with the floor.

Coming up, replace your heels on the floor as soon as you can, in the *demi-plié* position.

Take the same time to come up as you did to go down and make the whole movement smooth.

Grand plié in second position ★★★

★ Start in second position. Keep your back straight and your bottom down throughout the exercise.

As you bend your knees through the *demi-plié*, feel the weight between, not on, your feet.

In this *grand plié*, do not lift your heels. (This is also true for a *grand plié* in open fourth.)

Keep your back straight and knees out as you rise smoothly through the *demi-plié* position.

Make sure your feet do not roll onto their front edges at any point during the exercise.

Grand plié in fifth position ★★★

★ Fifth is the hardest position since your crossed feet only provide you with a small base.

Bend your knees into the *demi-plié* position, keeping your weight evenly over both your feet.

Stay lifted and do not sink onto your heels, even at the lowest point of the *plié*.

Replace your heels firmly in the *demi-plié* position as soon as possible as you come up.

The arm movements for *pliés* in all five positions of the feet are the same as shown here.

Battements tendus ★★★

Battements tendus means "stretched beatings". They use all the leg muscles and strengthen the feet and legs for footwork and travelling steps.

Slide your foot out along the floor, keeping it turned out.

Do the exercise *en croix* (see page 37). Here, it is shown to the front and side.

Pull your foot back in, keeping it in contact with the floor the whole time.

Keep your hips level as you stretch your leg out in each direction.

Pull your foot back in to first, ready to point to the back.

Ronds de jambe à terre ★★★

This means "circles of the leg on the ground". It improves turn-out. You draw a semi-circle with your foot, starting at the back (*en dehors*), as shown here, or the front (*en dedans*).

Start with your working leg pointed to second position.

Circle your foot until it is pointed to the back.

Your foot brushes to the front, through first position, at which point the foot is flat.

Point your foot to the front, ready to circle to the side again.

Keep your hips level and your legs turned out.

Your leg strikes the floor sharply, with a quality similar to striking a match.

Your foot starts flexed across the ankle of your supporting leg.

Stretch your foot until it is pointed and about 5cm (2in) off the floor.

Your foot does not touch the floor on its return.

Flex your foot behind your ankle, ready to strike to the side again.

Battements frappés ★★★

Frappé means "struck". This exercise is good preparation for jumping. You strike the floor with the ball of your foot.

Grands battements ★★★

This means "large beats". The movement builds strength, improves suppleness, balance and the height of your jumps. Do the exercise *en croix*.

★

Sweep your leg out and up off the floor, through *battement tendu*.

Keep both legs straight and your hips level throughout the exercise. Start in fifth position.

The upward sweep is strong and fast. The return is slightly more controlled.

As you raise your leg, keep your shoulders and arms relaxed.

Control your leg as you lower it so that it does not bump down on the ground.

Battements fondus ★★★

Fondu means "melted". The exercise builds strength and control. It is done *en croix*, and shown here to the front and the side.

★

Touch the shin of your supporting leg with the toe of your working leg.

Stretch both legs at the same time and raise your arm as you do so.

Keep your arm still as you bend your legs again.

Your arm moves to second as you stretch both legs.

Lower your arm to *bras bas* as you stretch to the back (not shown).

★

Draw your toe up to your knee. This position is called *retiré*.

Extend your leg to the highest possible point, keeping your knee turned out.

Lower your leg and close it through *battement tendu*.

Your arm closes at the same time as your leg.

Your arm follows the same route, whether your leg extends to the front, side or back.

Développés ★★★

This means "to unfold". *Développés* help you to control the leg and to produce a beautiful line. Do the exercise *en croix*.

Basic centre work

In the second part of the class you move into the middle of the studio to do exercises without the support of the *barre*. You can perform movements in the centre in five main positions, or alignments. These are called *croisé*, *ouvert*, *en face*, *écarté* and *éffacé*. They are designed so that an audience can see a clear outline of your body whatever direction you are facing.

Ouvert means "open". The leg nearest the front does not cross in front of your back leg.

Ecarté means "wide apart" or "thrown open". Your body makes a flat line.

Croisé means "crossed", because your legs look crossed to an audience when you face the corner.

Effacé means "obscured" or "turned away".

Facing the corner, your legs can be in fourth or fifth, or pointed in front or behind, with the leg nearest the back of the studio in front. Your arms can be in any position.

Your body faces one corner with your leg pointed to the other corner. Your arms are in fourth position with your head turned to look at your lifted arm.

En face means "facing the front". Your legs and arms can be in any position.

Your legs can be in fourth or fifth, or pointed to the front or behind, with the leg nearest the front of the studio in front. Your arms can be in any position.

Facing the corner, turn your head to the front of the studio and lift your upper back. Your arms are in fourth position. Your back leg is pointed to the corner.

Facing the corner

When you are asked to face the corner to do an exercise, imagine that you are standing inside a square. Face the corner of this square rather than the corner of the studio. This ensures that the front of the body can be seen clearly by a teacher or an audience, whatever the actual shape of the studio or stage.

The diagram shows the directions sixteen students face when asked to face the corner. They all face the corner of their own imaginary square.

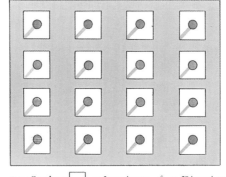

● = Student   ☐ = Imaginary square   ╱ = Direction faced

Adage steps

Some centre work exercises are known as *adage* steps. The word *adage* comes from the Italian *adagio*, meaning "at ease". In *adage* steps, one position flows smoothly into another. The *arabesque* on the opposite page is an example of an *adage* step.

Adage steps help to develop grace, balance and "line". (Line refers to the flowing curves which your body makes in ballet.) These steps also help to prepare female dancers for *pas de deux* work.

Ports de bras ★★★

Stand in fifth position, *croisé* (see page 42).

Raise your arms to first.

In *ports de bras* ("carriage of the arms"), the arms do not pass behind the line of the neck and shoulders. The neck stays relaxed and the arms move smoothly and freely, without disturbing the shoulders. Instead of holding the torso upright and facing the front, some exercises require you to turn or bend it slightly. This is called *epaulement* ("use of the shoulders"). It adds beauty to the lines made by the head, upper body and arms. You can see this below, when the arms are in fourth position. Lift the upper back slightly and turn your head to look over the raised arm.

Lower your back arm to second, then both to *bras bas*.

Raise your back arm to make fourth position again.

Raise your arms to fifth, keeping them smoothly curved.

Lower your arms to second, without letting your elbows droop.

★

Then lower both arms together back down to *bras bas*.

Raise your arms smoothly through first position again.

Lift your front arm and take your back arm to the side, to fourth position.

Lower your front arm until your arms are in second position.

Arabesques ★★★

Stand in fifth position, *ouvert* (see page 42).

Do a *demi-plié* and start to raise your arms to first.

In an *arabesque*, your body makes a long line from the raised foot, along the leg and up the back to the shoulder. The raised leg is held directly behind your body. Your arms can be in any position, although in a Classical *arabesque*, as shown here, one arm is always stretched out in front. The line continues along it to the ends of your fingers. The pictures show a sequence which progresses through first *arabesque à terre* ("on the ground"), first *arabesque en l'air* ("in the air"), *arabesque penchée* ("leaning *arabesque*") and third *arabesque*. Your arms move smoothly through the positions shown in the pictures.

Lower your arms and close your legs in fifth position.

Third *arabesque*

Lower your leg to the floor, bringing your left arm to the front.

★

Lift your back leg, keeping your hips level, head up and torso upright.

Continue to lift your leg and tilt your body. Keep your upper back supported.

Smoothly slide your front foot out to fourth position.

As you straighten both legs, transfer your weight to your front foot and move your arms as shown.

Return your leg to its *en l'air* position, lifting your upper back as you do so.

First *arabesque à terre*

First *arabesque en l'air*

Arabesque penchée

A pirouette en dehors ★★★

Starting position.

★

Point to the right, taking your arms out to second.

Demi-plié in fifth and bring your right arm in to third.

About pirouettes

A *pirouette* is a turn or a spin. It can be done at any speed, on *pointe* or on *demi-pointe* (tip-toe). There are two directions for a turn: *en dehors* (to the outside) and *en dedans* (to the inside). For a turn *en dehors* you turn away from your supporting leg. For a turn *en dedans*, you turn the other way.

Relevé (see below) into *pirouette* position, turning to the right. Whip your left arm into first position.

Keep on turning to your right.

Make one full turn to face the front again.

Close your right leg behind, in *demi-plié*. Arms move down to *demi-bras*.

Straighten your legs and lower your arms.

Pirouette position

In *pirouette* position, the toes of the working leg touch just under the knee of the supporting leg. This position is reached by a movement called a *relevé*. This starts from a *demi-plié*, followed by a strong rise to *demi-pointe* on one foot, with the other leg drawn up to the knee.

A pirouette en dedans ★★★

Starting position.

★

Point to the front and raise your arms to first position.

Lunge forward and move your left arm out to third.

Bring your left leg into *pirouette* position and left arm into first. Turn to your right.

Keep turning, making one and a quarter turns.

Spotting

Dancers use a technique called spotting to stop them from getting dizzy during *pirouettes*. They fix their eyes on one point for as long as possible during the turn, and then flick their head around to look at the same point over the other shoulder to complete the circle.

Finish facing the right front corner.

Close your left leg in front, in *demi-plié*. Bring your arms down to first position.

Straighten your legs and lower your arms.

A glissade ★★★

Glissades are gliding steps. They are usually used to link other steps. You can do *glissades* in any direction. Below, the black spot shows where the dancer started from, to show how the step travels.

Start in fifth position with your right foot in front.

Do a *demi-plié*. Your arms stay in *bras bas*.

Slide your front foot to the right, pointed and just off the floor. Raise your arms to *demi-seconde*.

Transfer your weight and point your left foot, just off the floor.

Close your left foot behind, in fifth position.

A pas de bourrée piqué under ★★★

There are several sorts of *bourrées*. Most consist of fast, tiny steps. *Piqué* means "pricked" and this step is performed as if the floor is hot. It is usually danced on *pointe* but for practice it can be done as shown, on *demi-pointe*.

Start in fifth position with your left foot in front.

Bend your left leg and pick up your right foot. Your arms move to third, passing through first.

Step onto your right leg on *demi-pointe*, without travelling. Pick up your left foot in front. Your arms move to second position.

Take a tiny step to the side, picking up your right foot in front.

Finish in *fondu*. Your right arm comes to third position.

A pas de bourrée under ★★★

The sequence below shows a step called a *pas de bourrée* under, because one leg stretches out and closes behind, or "under", the other.

Start in fifth position with your right foot in front.

As you bend your left leg, slide the right foot out, and point it just off the floor. Arms go to *demi-seconde*.

Close your right leg behind in fifth on *demi-pointe*. Your legs are straight.

Take a small step to the left and close your right leg in front of the left.

Demi-plié in fifth position. Your arms return to *bras bas*.

Jumps and travelling steps

This part of the class consists of *allegro* steps. *Allegro* is an Italian musical term meaning quick and lively. Most *allegro* steps are jumps. They require stamina and accuracy. There are three kinds of *allegro* steps, called *petit allegro*, *allegro* and *grand allegro*. The names refer to jumps that increase in size. There are some *petit allegro* steps shown opposite. On pages 48-49 are some *allegro* and *grand allegro* steps.

The height of a jump is called its elevation.

This *grand allegro* jump is called a *grand jeté en avant*.

Internet link
For a link to a website where you can see animated figures demonstrating advanced steps, go to **www.usborne-quicklinks.com**

Your arms should look relaxed and graceful during a jump.

Keep your upper body lifted during a jump. This will help you to land quietly.

If a *grand allegro* jump is performed well, there is a moment when the body seems to be suspended in the air.

In most jumps, the right arm is pointed up or out in front when the left leg is leading, and *vice versa*. This is known as "opposition".

Your feet are strongly pointed in the air.

Performing jumps

When you do a jump, don't let your arms flap about with the effort of getting yourself up into the air. Try to make the jump look as neat, controlled and effortless as possible without losing the vitality of the step. Look up slightly and focus ahead, raising your arms at the same time as you spring off the ground for a jump. The upward movement helps to make your body feel and look light, and helps your elevation.

Taking off and landing

It is important to take off and land from a jump correctly, otherwise you can damage your bones and joints. Start a jump from a *demi-plié* (see page 39). This helps you to get a strong spring into the air. Push into the ground with your toes as your foot starts to lift. Point your toes as soon as they leave the floor. As you land, your toes touch the ground first and your heel touches last. Bend your knees to absorb the shock and land smoothly and quietly.

A changement ★★★

Changement means "change". It is a warm-up jump starting from fifth position with one foot in front, changing your feet in the air, to finish with your other foot in front, in fifth position.

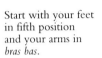

★

Jump into the air and change your legs so that the other leg is in front.

Start with your feet in fifth position and your arms in *bras bas*.

Bend both knees in a *demi-plié*, to prepare for the jump.

Land in fifth, in *demi-plié*. This absorbs the shock of the landing.

Straighten your legs. Your arms stay relaxed throughout.

An échappé sauté ★★★

Échappé means "escaped" and *sauté* means "jump". This warm-up jump goes from fifth position to second and back to fifth with the other leg in front.

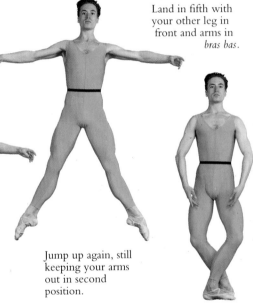

★

Land with feet and arms in second position. Don't let your feet get too wide.

Land in fifth with your other leg in front and arms in *bras bas*.

Start in fifth position. *Demi-plié* to prepare to jump.

Keep the same leg in front as you jump. Your arms move up to first position.

Jump up again, still keeping your arms out in second position.

A pas de chat ★★★

Pas de chat ("step of the cat") is a *petit allegro* jump. It requires control and balance. You start in fifth position.

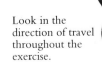

★

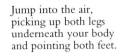

Look in the direction of travel throughout the exercise.

Lift your back foot to the back of your calf. Bend your other knee.

Jump into the air, picking up both legs underneath your body and pointing both feet.

Land on a bent leg. Your other leg points to the mid-shin.

Close in fifth with the same foot in front as before.

An assemblé over ★★★

An *assemblé* (assembled) step is an *allegro* step. It can be done in any direction. You jump from one leg, but land on both feet. In an *assemblé* over, you change the legs so that you land with the other leg in front.

Start in fifth position with your right leg in front. Do a *demi-plié*.

★

Swish your back leg out, to about 5cm (2in) off the floor.

Jump, stretching your right leg beneath you. Your left leg lifts to help you gain height.

Bring both legs together in the air with your left leg in front.

Land in *demi-plié* and straighten your legs. The step does not travel.

A sissonne fermé en avant ★★★

The name of this *allegro* step means "to scissor, close and move forward". To do a *sissonne*, you jump from both feet and land on one foot.

★

Start with your left foot in front, facing the left-hand corner.

Do a *demi-plié* to prepare to jump, moving in the direction of the corner.

Your arms move to *demi-seconde*. Your right leg stretches behind into *arabesque*.

Land on a bent left leg with your right leg still stretched behind.

Close your right leg behind in fifth. Your arms move down to *bras bas*.

★

Start in fifth position with your right leg in front. Do a *demi-plié*.

Jump up, beating your right leg to the back and hiding it behind your left leg.

While your legs are still stretched, bring your right leg to the front again.

Land in fifth position in a *demi-plié*.

Stretch your legs to finish the movement.

Batterie ★★★

Batterie is a beating movement of the legs in the air. This *batterie* step is an *entrechat quatre*. Your legs cross twice.

These two *grand allegro* jumps are called *grands jetés*. The dancer splits the legs in the air and lands on one foot.

★

In *grands jetés*, the arms can be held in different positions.

★

This *grand allegro* jump is called a *temps de poisson* ("fish step").

★

Grand allegro

These large jumps should look effortless. You can disguise the force used to gain height by keeping your arms looking supported but relaxed and your upper body steady. The landing should be soft. For these jumps you need space and you must be well warmed up. It is safest to work on them under supervision in a class.

Grand allegro in performance

Most principal male roles contain dramatic *grand allegro* leaps. Some female roles, such as the Queen of the Wilis in *Giselle*, also require dynamic *grand allegro*.

Pointe work ★★★

For females, the class may end with *pointe* work. The exercise below, an *échappé relevé*, is a warm-up for *pointe* work. It exercises and strengthens the feet. *Echappé* means "escaped" and *relevé* means "lifted". The legs separate sharply into second position, either on *demi-pointe* as shown below, or on *pointe*. Don't attempt the on *pointe* version unless you have previously worked on it in class.

In an *échappé relevé en pointe* (left), there is a very slight spring at the last moment in order to rise onto the toes. The feet stay just in contact with the ground, though.

★

Start the exercise in fifth position with your right foot in front and your arms held in *bras bas*.

Do a *demi-plié* in preparation to shoot your legs apart. You need to support your upper body.

Your toes stay lightly in contact with the ground as your legs separate and straighten.

Bring your feet back into fifth position in a *demi-plié* with your left leg in front and arms in *bras bas*.

Shoot your legs out again. Do a sequence of *échappés relevés*, changing your feet each time.

A short *enchainement*

Your teacher might combine movements to make an *enchainement* (a "linking"). The *enchainement* below is performed to two sets of four counts, so you need to count steadily "one... two... three... four" twice over. The numbers below the pictures show where you should be at each count. Each count takes up the same amount of time.

Glissade derrière	
Assemblé derrière	
Pas de chat	
Changement	

The sequence consists of the four movements above.

Stand still for the first three counts.

1... 2... 3...

Start in fifth with your right foot in front and your arms in *bras bas*.

4...

Demi-plié on the fourth count. The next two stages take place fairly quickly.

Swish your left foot to the side, just off the floor. Raise your arms to first position.

Transfer your weight to your left foot, taking a big step to the left as you do so.

★
★★★

On the count of one, close your right leg in front of the left, in *demi-plié*.

1...

Swish your back (left) leg out, to about 5cm (2in) off the floor. Your arms move to *demi-seconde*.

Jump, stretching your right leg beneath you. Your left leg lifts a bit but the jump does not travel.

Bring both legs together in the air with your right leg still in front.

2...

Land in fifth, in a *demi-plié*, with your right leg in front. Raise your arms to third and look to the left.

Lift your back (left) leg to the knee and prepare to spring into the air.

Bring your arms down, look to the front and change your legs in the air.

In the air, make sure both legs are fully picked up underneath you.

Land on a bent left leg, bringing your pointed right foot into your mid-shin.

3...

Close your right leg in front of your left leg, in a *demi-plié* in fifth position.

4...

Repeat the sequence, starting with your left foot in front. This time, travel to the right.

Training for *pas de deux*

Pas de deux is usually taught in full-time ballet schools after the dancers have been thoroughly trained in all other aspects of technique. The qualities required of the male and female are different but equally demanding. A boy must have the strength to lift the girl without overbalancing or dropping her. Girls need balance as well as strength in the feet and legs and in the wrists for hand grips.

This hold comes from a late 20th century ballet.

This type of hold is called a straight lift. It does not travel.

Early training

Most of a girl's early training for *pas de deux* involves practice to develop her balance. She also needs to produce a graceful and expressive line with her body. *Adage* steps (see page 42) are good for developing line. Early training for male dancers includes weight-lifting to build strength. This is carefully regulated so that boys do not develop bulky muscles which would spoil their streamlined appearance and slow them down.

This is a Classical *pas de deux* hold, from *The Sleeping Beauty*.

Pas de deux work should look effortless and neither partner should show any strain.

Types of hold

Straight lift: the man stands on one spot and propels the female straight up into the air.

Travelling lift: the female dancer starts with a jump. Her partner lifts her and carries her, setting her down some distance away.

Supported balance: the female stands on one leg on *pointe*. The male supports her by her hand, elbow or waist and adjusts her balance if necessary.

This type of position is called a supported balance.

Internet link
For a link to a website where you can read more about *pas de deux*, go to **www.usborne-quicklinks.com**

Some famous dancers

You can find lots more information about these dancers on the Internet. For links to recommended websites, go to **www.usborne-quicklinks.com** and enter the keyword "ballet".

Carlos Acosta (born 1973) is Cuban and known for his technical virtuosity. He dances with several different companies including The Royal Ballet, where he is a principal guest artist. He has also choreographed a work, combining ballet and Cuban dance, which is based on his life story.

Mikhail Baryshnikov (born 1948) studied at the Kirov Ballet School. He left Russia to join The Royal Ballet. In 1975, he joined the American Ballet Theatre and was its director throughout the 1980s. He is famous for leaps and turns.

Erik Bruhn (1928-1986) was Danish. He joined the Royal Danish Ballet in 1947 and danced with many companies worldwide. He was an excellent technician who also directed.

Margot Fonteyn in her role as Odette in *Swan Lake* in 1951.

Anton Dolin (1904-1983), an English dancer, was spotted by Diaghilev and appeared with the Ballets Russes. In 1928, he began a famous partnership with Alicia Markova. Later in life, he turned to choreography and directing.

Anthony Dowell (born 1943) trained at the Royal Ballet School and joined the company in 1962. He was well known for his long partnership with Antoinette Sibley. He was Director of The Royal Ballet from 1986 to 2001.

Viviana Durante (born 1967) is from Rome. She attended the Royal Ballet School, then joined The Royal Ballet, where she was a principal during the 1990s. She now dances all over the world.

Suzanne Farrell (born 1945) trained at the School of American Ballet. At age 16 she was introduced to the New York City Ballet by George Balanchine, who created many roles for her. She founded her own company in 2000.

Viviana Durante in her costume for *Rubies*.

Darcey Bussell (born 1969) is from London and studied at the Royal Ballet School. She joined Sadler's Wells Royal Ballet, then moved to The Royal Ballet, becoming a principal in 1989. She has danced all the major roles.

Alina Cojocaru (born 1981) is from Romania. She rose fast through the ranks of The Royal Ballet, becoming a principal in 2001. She has danced all the major roles.

Adam Cooper (born 1972) is from London and joined The Royal Ballet in 1989, becoming a principal in 1994. He left to join Adventures in Motion Pictures after starring in their version of *Swan Lake*. He now dances as a guest artist with The Royal Ballet and stars in musicals. He also choreographs.

Alexandra Danilova (1904-1997) danced with the Imperial Russian Ballet until joining the Ballets Russes in 1924. She later danced mostly in the USA, where her elegant performances were hugely popular.

Margot Fonteyn (1919-1991) studied at Sadler's Wells, becoming a soloist at 16. She was known for two long partnerships, with Michael Somes and Rudolf Nureyev. She created many roles and held the rare honorary title *Prima Ballerina Assoluta*.

Sylvie Guillem (born 1965) is from Paris and trained at the Paris Opéra Ballet School. She is a principal guest artist with The Royal Ballet and dances all over the world. She is well known for amazing athleticism.

Marcia Haydée (born 1939), a Brazilian dancer, worked under the direction of John Cranko at the Stuttgart Ballet. With her dramatic flair, she created many leading roles. She was Artistic Director at Stuttgart from 1976 to 1995.

Robert Helpmann (1909-1986) was an Australian who danced with the Sadler's Wells Ballet in the 1930s and 40s. He had great dramatic ability. Later, he choreographed for and directed the Australian Ballet.

Tamara Karsavina (1885-1978) contributed enormously to the success of the Ballets Russes. In 1918, she married an Englishman, later becoming a great influence on English ballet.

Serge Lifar (1905-1986) trained under Nijinska. He joined the Ballets Russes, where he was one of Diaghilev's last great male dancers. He later joined the Paris Opéra. He also choreographed.

Natalia Makarova (born 1941) made her debut with the Kirov Ballet and then joined the American Ballet Theatre in 1970. There was a fragile quality to her dancing which made her excel in roles such as Giselle.

Alicia Markova (1910-2004) joined the Ballets Russes at 14. She helped to form several companies, including the London Festival Ballet. She later became Director at the Metropolitan Opera House in New York.

Vaslav Nijinsky in *L'Oiseau d'Or* from *Le Festin* performed in Paris in 1909.

Arthur Mitchell (born 1934) went to the School of American Ballet at a time when black Classical dancers were rare. He became a principal with the New York City Ballet and later founded the Dance Theatre of Harlem.

Irek Mukhamedov (born 1960) was a leading dancer with the Bolshoi Ballet in the 1980s and with The Royal Ballet in the 1990s. He is well known for his dramatic skill.

Vaslav Nijinsky (1880-1950) first appeared with the Imperial Russian Ballet and then joined the Ballets Russes, for which he choreographed. His career was cut short by mental illness.

Rudolf Nureyev (1938-1993) made his debut with the Kirov Ballet. In 1961, he left Russia to join The Royal Ballet, where he became the leading male dancer. From 1983 to 1991, he was Director of the Paris Opéra.

Anna Pavlova (1881-1935) was one of the first stars of the Ballets Russes. She toured the world with her own company and is best known for her solo of *The Dying Swan*.

Tamara Rojo (born 1974) is from Spain. She has danced a huge variety of roles all over the world. In 2000, she joined The Royal Ballet, becoming a principal in 2002.

Peter Schaufuss (born 1949) made his debut aged eight with the Danish Royal Ballet. He was a principal with the New York City Ballet before directing first the English National Ballet, then the Royal Danish Ballet. In 1997 he formed his own company.

Lynn Seymour (born 1939) is Canadian and danced with The Royal Ballet. Kenneth MacMillan created roles for her.

Antoinette Sibley (born 1939) joined The Royal Ballet in 1956 and was the first to dance a lead role without first becoming a principal. She and Dowell were known as "the Golden Pair" because they were so well matched.

Wayne Sleep (born 1948) joined The Royal Ballet in 1966. He became a principal in 1973, and danced many character roles. In 1980, he set up Dash, his own dance company. He also dances in musicals.

Galina Ulanova (1910-1998) joined the Kirov Ballet in 1928. She was a supremely graceful dance-actress.

Miyako Yoshida (born 1965) is Japanese. She joined The Royal Ballet as a principal in 1995.

Rudolf Nureyev

Some famous choreographers

You can find lots more information about these choreographers on the Internet. For links to recommended websites, go to **www.usborne-quicklinks.com** and enter the keyword "ballet".

19th century

Auguste Bournonville (1805-1879) was Danish and his father was his first teacher. In 1820, he studied under Vestris in Paris, who taught the elegant French style of the 18th century. He became a soloist at the Paris Opéra, but in 1829 returned to Denmark to become Ballet Master to the Royal Danish Ballet. He remained in this post for 47 years. His repertory has been preserved to this day in Denmark. He created numerous ballets; including *Napoli* (1842), *A Folk Tale* (1854), a reworking of *La Sylphide* (1832) and *Konservatoriet* (1849) – a recreation of a class with Vestris.
See also page 9.

Lev Ivanov (1834-1901) trained in St. Petersburg and Moscow and was both a character dancer and Petipa's Assistant Ballet Master at the same time. Though overshadowed by Petipa, he did choreograph the important Acts 2 and 4 in *Swan Lake*, and the first version of *The Nutcracker* (1892). He also choreographed a new version of *La Fille Mal Gardée* (1885).
See also page 11.

Jules Perrot (1810-1892) started his career as a dancer in popular theatrical shows in Paris but gave this up to study seriously with Vestris. He began dancing at the Paris Opéra in 1830 and became an amazing dancer, who performed with Marie Taglioni. In 1835, he went on a tour of Europe, choreographing his own ballets. Carlotta Grisi became his protégée and he returned to the Paris Opéra to choreograph her dances in *Giselle* (1841). He later worked in London and St. Petersburg, where sections of his choreography have been preserved. His ballets include *Ondine* (1834), *La Esmerelda* (1844) and *Catarina* (1846).

Marius Petipa (1818-1910) was born into a dancing family and studied with his father, then with Vestris at the Paris Opéra, where Petipa's brother was a famous dancer. He performed and choreographed in France and Spain before going to St. Petersburg as a dancer in 1847. In 1869, he became Ballet Master there and created ballets which combined technical brilliance with great spectacle. He strengthened the technique of the Imperial Russian Ballet and its school, creating the foremost company of the time. His ballets include *Don Quixote* (1869), *La Bayadère* (1877), *The Sleeping Beauty* (1890), *Swan Lake* (1895) and *Raymonda* (1898).
See also page 11.

Arthur St. Léon (1821-1870) was born in Paris and trained with his father who was Ballet Master in Stuttgart. He worked as a dancer and choreographer all over Europe, becoming Ballet Master in St. Petersburg as well as Paris. He was married to the ballerina Fanny Cerrito and his masterpiece is *Coppélia* (1870).

Early 20th century

Mikhail Fokine (1880-1942) graduated into the Imperial Ballet at the Maryinsky Theatre in St. Petersburg in 1898 as a soloist. He was an impressive dancer, who later worked for Diaghilev as a choreographer. The ballets he created for the Ballets Russes rebelled against the conventions of the late 19th century story ballet. It is these that he became most famous for. From 1922, he worked in America, dancing, staging ballets and teaching. His works include *The Firebird* (1910), *Schéhérazade* (1910), *Petrushka* (1911) and *Le Spectre de la Rose* (1912).
See also page 12.

Leonide Massine (1895-1979) was born in Moscow and graduated into the Bolshoi Company in 1912. His talent was spotted by Diaghilev, who also encouraged him to choreograph. His early works were one-act story ballets with many characters. In the 1930s, he created "symphonic" ballets – abstract works to existing symphonic music. His ballets include *La Boutique Fantasque* (1919) and *Choreartium* (1933).

Bronislava Nijinska (1891-1972) was Nijinsky's sister. She graduated into the Maryinsky Company in St. Petersburg and later joined the Ballets Russes. She helped Diaghilev revive *The Sleeping Beauty* in London in 1912, after which she choreographed for him. Her later career was spent in South America, Paris and London, where she worked for the Markova-Dolin Company. Her ballets include *Renard* (1922) and *Bolero* (1928).
See also page 12.

Late 20th century

Frederick Ashton (1904-1988) grew up in Peru, where he was inspired to become a dancer after watching Anna Pavlova. In London, he became a pupil of Marie Rambert who encouraged him to choreograph. His theme ballets include *Jazz Calender* (1968) and *Les Rendezvous* (1933). His story ballets include *Cinderella* (1948) and *La Fille Mal Gardée* (1960). His abstract masterpieces include *Symphonic Variations* (1946), *Scènes de Ballet* (1948) and *Monotones* (1965).
See also pages 12 and 15.

George Balanchine (1904-1983) trained as both a dancer and a musician in St. Petersburg and joined the State Company in 1921, starting to choreograph at age 18. At age 20, he left Russia to join Diaghilev as a dancer and ballet master. He is famous for founding the American style of Classical ballet. He also choreographed for musicals. His works include *Serenade* (1934) and *Agon* (1957).
See also pages 12 and 15.

Maurice Béjart (born 1927) comes from France and started his career in Paris and London. He danced and choreographed for several companies before founding a company in Brussels in 1960 called the Ballet of the 20th Century. The company later moved to Lausanne. He is known for creating different and surprising work. His ballets include *Nijinsky – Clown of God* (1979).

David Bintley (born 1957) comes from England and showed a talent for choreography and character roles while training at the Royal Ballet School. He became director of Birmingham Royal Ballet in 1995. His ballets include *Still Life at the Penguin Café* (1988), *Hobson's Choice* (1989), *Edward II* (1995) and *The Nutcracker Sweeties* (1996).

Matthew Bourne (born 1960) grew up in London. He was inspired by musicals but didn't start dancing until he was 22. He was Artistic Director and Choreographer of the innovative dance company Adventures in Motion Pictures from 1987 onwards, then founded New Adventures in 2002. His works include the ground-breaking *Swan Lake* (1995), in which the swans are danced by men, *Cinderella* (1997) and *Play Without Words* (2002). He also choreographs for musicals.

Christopher Bruce (born 1945) became a dancer with the Ballet Rambert and was outstanding in intense, dramatic roles. He began to choreograph in 1969 and was Artistic Director of the Ballet Rambert from 1994 to 2002. His famous works include *Ancient Voices of Children* (1975), *Cruel Garden* (1977) and *Ghost Dances* (1981).

John Cranko (1927-1973) was born in South Africa. He joined Sadler's Wells Royal Ballet in 1946 and worked with The Royal Ballet, also creating ballets for companies all over the world. He then became Director of the Stuttgart Ballet. He also choreographed musicals. His works include *Pineapple Poll* (1951) and *The Taming of the Shrew* (1969). See also page 15.

Ninette de Valois (1898-2001) danced in pier shows and pantomimes as a child. After working for Diaghilev's Ballets Russes, she founded the Vic-Wells Ballet, the forerunner of The Royal Ballet and Birmingham Royal Ballet. Her ballets include *Job* (1931), *The Rake's Progress* (1935) and *Checkmate* (1937). See also page 15.

William Forsythe (born 1949) was born in the USA. He choreographed for the Stuttgart Ballet before becoming Director of Frankfurt Ballet from 1984 to 2004. His style is very athletic and he often uses electronic music. His abstract works include *Septext* (1985), *In the middle, somewhat elevated* (1988) and *Herman Scherman* (1992).

Jiri Kylian (born 1947) is a Czech who studied in Prague, as well as at the Royal Ballet School. He joined the Stuttgart Ballet in 1968 and worked under John Cranko, where he began to choreograph. He was Artistic Director of Nederlands Dans Theater from 1976 to 1999. His style is very energetic and contemporary and his best known works include *Symphony of Psalms* (1978).

Kenneth MacMillan (1929-1992) trained at the Sadler's Wells Ballet School and joined the company in 1946. Though he was a fine Classical dancer, he preferred choreography to performing and built up an early reputation. In 1958, he created *The Burrow* for Lynn Seymour, who later became the inspiration for much of his work. MacMillan was well-known for presenting difficult subjects, such as violence and war, and was also keen on directing drama. He died backstage at the Royal Opera House, London, during a performance of one of his works. His ballets include *The Invitation* (1960), *Romeo and Juliet* (1965), *Manon* (1974), *Mayerling* (1978), *Gloria* (1980), *The Prince of the Pagodas* (1989) and *Winter Dreams* (1991).
See also page 15.

John Neumeier (born 1942) is an American dancer, choreographer and director. He studied in America and also at the Royal Ballet School. He danced with the Stuttgart Ballet and became director at the Frankfurt Ballet in 1969. In 1973, he moved to the Hamburg Ballet. His best known ballets are *Separate Journeys* (1968), *Frontiers* (1969), *Rondo* (1970), *Don Juan* (1972), *A Midsummer Night's Dream* (1977) and *St. Matthew Passion* (1981).

Jerome Robbins (1918-1998) was born in America and began working as a dancer in musicals. He joined the American Ballet Theatre in 1940. His first ballet *Fancy Free* (1944), about sailors on leave in New York, was a great success. He choreographed for New York City Ballet as well as for Broadway shows such as *West Side Story*. His best known ballets are *Afternoon of a Faun* (1953) and *Dances at a Gathering* (1969).

Glen Tetley (born 1926) is an American who has danced for many different companies and choreographed for most of the major companies in the world. His works include *Pierrot Lunaire* (1962), *Summer's End* (1980) and *Alice* (1986), based on the stories of Lewis Carroll. See also page 15.

Twyla Tharp (born 1942) is an American dancer who studied contemporary choreography before joining the Paul Taylor Dance Company in 1963. She formed her own company two years later. Though she is a contemporary choreographer, she has created works for the American Ballet Theatre, including *Push Comes to Shove* (1976) and *In An Upper Room* (1987).

Antony Tudor (1909-1987) did not start dancing until he was 19. He had a strong stage presence. He worked with many companies – first his own London Ballet, also the Royal Swedish Ballet, New York City Ballet and The Royal Ballet. His works include *Lilac Garden* (1936), *Pillar of Fire* (1942) and *Echoing of Trumpets* (1963).

Hans Van Manen (born 1932) is Dutch and has a close association with Nederlands Dans Theater. His ballets include *Grosse Fuge* (1971), *Twilight* (1972) and *5 Tangos* (1977).

Christopher Wheeldon (born 1973) is English. A former dancer, he choreographs works for many companies but chiefly for New York City Ballet. His ballets include *Polyphonia* (2001), *Continuum* (2002) and *Tryst* (2002).

Ballet stories

On the Internet, you can find more ballet stories, performance details and background information, and listen to clips of ballet music. For links to recommended websites, go to **www.usborne-quicklinks.com**

Early 19th century ballets

La Sylphide
date: 1836
choreography: Bournonville after Taglioni (1832)
music: Lovenskjold

James, a Scottish farmer, is due to be married to Effie, but is besotted by a sylph who appears in his farmhouse. At his wedding celebrations, she entices him into the forest. An old witch, Madge, who James sent away from the wedding, prepares a poisoned scarf, with which she intends to take her revenge. Madge tells James the magic scarf will make the sylph belong to him always, but instead it kills her. James dies of grief and Effie finds happiness by marrying another farmer.

Giselle
date: 1841
choreography: Coralli and Perrot
music: Adam

A nobleman, Count Albrecht, disguises himself as a villager in order to court a peasant girl, Giselle. She loves dancing with him, but her mother prefers her to marry Hilarion, a woodcutter. On the day Giselle is crowned queen in a local celebration, a hunting party of nobles arrives. Hilarion discovers that the Duke's daughter Bathilde is Albrecht's real fiancée. He tells Giselle, who goes insane and kills herself with Albrecht's sword.

Giselle is buried in the forest. At midnight, the ghosts of girls who have died before their wedding day, called the Wilis, summon her to dance with them. Myrtha, their queen, is full of vengeance: any man she sees is made to dance until he dies. Hilarion is her first victim and when Albrecht comes to lay flowers on Giselle's grave, she commands him to dance. Giselle still loves him and by dancing with him saves him from dying of exhaustion. At dawn, the power of the Wilis melts away and Giselle returns to her grave, leaving Albrecht sorrowing and alone.

Late 19th century ballets

Don Quixote
date: 1869
choreography: Petipa
music: Minkus

A Spaniard called Don Quixote is obsessed by stories of medieval knights. He decides that he wants to be one, so he arms himself and sets off to seek adventure.

Meanwhile in Barcelona, a girl named Kitri is being forced by her father to marry rich Gamache, instead of Basilio, the man she really loves. Don Quixote arrives at Kitri's father's inn and believes that she is his ideal love. He challenges Gamache to a duel in the hope of winning her, but is chased away.

To win Kitri, Basilio pretends to kill himself and begs Kitri's father with a dying wish for her hand in marriage. His request is granted and he stops pretending that he is going to die and the lovers marry and run away.

Don Quixote sees a knight who is protecting a young maiden. Thinking that the maiden is his ideal love again, Don Quixote challenges the knight to a duel, but is defeated. The knight turns out to be Basilio and the maiden is Kitri. The pair of lovers perform a final grand *pas de deux*. Don Quixote then leaves in search of further adventures.

Coppélia
date: 1870
choreography: St. Léon
music: Delibes

A toymaker named Dr. Coppélius sets his latest doll, Coppélia, on his balcony. She is so realistic that Franz falls in love with her. His fiancée, Swanhilda, is very annoyed, so she creeps inside the shop and realizes that Coppélia is only a clockwork doll. Suddenly, the doctor returns, so she hides with Coppélia and dresses in her clothes.

Franz breaks in to look for Coppélia, but the doctor seizes him and drugs him. He plans to transfer the life from Franz into Coppélia to make her come alive.

Swanhilda impersonates Coppélia and tricks the doctor into believing that he has suceeded. She rescues Franz and shows Dr. Coppélius that his doll is not really alive at all.

At the festival to celebrate the town's new bell, Swanhilda apologizes to Dr. Coppélius. She and Franz dance in the *divertissements* which show the uses that the new bell will be put to, such as chiming the hours and calling people to work, to prayer and to war.

La Bayadère
date: 1877
choreography: Petipa
music: Minkus

Solor, a young Indian warrior, is in love with Nikiya, one of the dancers of the temple who are called the Bayadères. However, the local ruler, the Grand Brahmin, wants Nikiya for himself. Then Solor sees Gamsatti, the daughter of the Rajah, and becomes engaged to her. At the dances to celebrate the betrothal, Nikiya is made to dance. A basket of flowers arrives for her, which she thinks is from Solor, but really it has been sent from the Rajah and Gamsatti. The basket conceals a poisonous snake, which bites Nikiya. The Grand Brahmin offers her an antidote to the poison, on the condition that she will be his. However, she refuses it, preferring to die and remain true to Solor.

Smoking on an opium pipe, Solor dreams of Nikiya in the famous Kingdom of the Shades scene. At the wedding of Solor and Gamsatti, the temple is struck by lightning and everyone is killed. In the final scene, Solor and Nikiya are reunited for eternity.

The Sleeping Beauty
date: 1890
choreography: Petipa
music: Tchaikovsky

At the christening of Princess Aurora, all the fairies in the land have been invited to come and bring gifts for her. However, a wicked fairy named Carabosse had been forgotten. In revenge, she declares in a mime scene that on her 16th birthday, Aurora will prick her finger on the spindle of a spinning wheel and die.

The good Lilac Fairy cannot break this spell, but she lessens it by saying that Aurora will not die, but sleep for a hundred years.' Then a handsome prince will wake her with a kiss. To prevent this from happening, the King bans all spinning wheels from the land.

At Aurora's 16th birthday party, four princes come to seek her hand in marriage and dance the famous Rose Adage with her. When she sees a strange woman with a spindle, Aurora is fascinated as she has never seen one before. Before anyone can stop her, she pricks her finger and the whole court falls asleep. Over the years, a forest grows around the palace.

One hundred years later, a prince is hunting in this same forest. Downcast, he is seeking his ideal love and sends his companions away in order to be alone. The Lilac Fairy appears and shows the prince a vision of Aurora. Enchanted and guided by the Lilac Fairy, he finds his way to where she sleeps, fights off Carabosse and wakens Aurora with a kiss. At their wedding, characters from other fairy tales, such as Red Riding Hood and Puss in Boots, come to celebrate the marriage.

The Nutcracker
date: 1892
choreography: Ivanov
music: Tchaikovsky

In the original version of this ballet, a little girl named Clara is given a nutcracker doll by a strange magician named Drosselmeyer at a Christmas party. At night, Clara creeps downstairs to find her doll and watches in amazement as the Christmas tree grows and toy soldiers fight a battle against rats. She helps the Nutcracker, the leader of the soldiers, by knocking down the Rat King with her shoe.

As a reward, the Nutcracker takes her on a magical journey through a land of snow, where snowflakes dance, and into the Kingdom of Sweets. Here, Clara is entertained by a *divertissement* of dancing sweets, ending in a wonderful *pas de deux* for the Sugar Plum Fairy and the Nutcracker Prince. Suddenly, Clara is back at home, clutching her doll. Was it all a dream?

Swan Lake
date: 1895
choreography: Petipa and Ivanov
music: Tchaikovsky

Prince Siegfried is being heavily persuaded by his mother the Queen to choose a bride. However, he is more interested in a swan-hunting expedition because it is his birthday and his companions have presented him with a crossbow.

At a lakeside by moonlight, he is astonished to see a swan change into a beautiful maiden. The maiden, Princess Odette, is terrified of Siegfried at first, but then tells him her story in a mime sequence.

By day, she and her companions have been turned into swans by a wicked magician called Von Rothbart. Only at night can they become human. The spell can only be broken if someone swears to love and marry her. Siegfried believes he has found his true love and swears to be faithful to Odette.

Siegfried's mother organizes a ball, so that he will meet a princess to marry. Von Rothbart arrives in disguise, bringing his daughter Odile. He has disguised her to look like Odette and Siegfried is tricked into asking her to marry him. At the lake, Odette is grieving as now the spell can never be broken. Siegfried arrives full of remorse and Odette forgives him. They decide that the only thing to do is to die together and they plunge into the lake. A final scene shows them united for eternity.

Raymonda
date: 1898
choreography: Petipa
music: Glazunov

Raymonda celebrates her birthday. Her fiancé Jean de Brienne, who is due to arrive at the castle the next day, sends her a gift of his portrait.

A Saracen warrior named Abderaman arrives at the castle where she lives and tries to win Raymonda's love. At night, she dreams that Jean comes down from his portrait and dances with her. She wakes to find Abderaman there beside her instead, in an attempt to renew his advances.

Raymonda awaits Jean anxiously. Meanwhile, Abderaman invites her to dance and he and his companions try to kidnap her. Just in time, Jean enters with his brother, the King of Hungary. Jean fights a duel with Abderaman and is victorious. At last Raymonda is safe and she marries Jean. A great feast is held at the castle to celebrate their wedding.

Early 20th century ballets

The Firebird
date: 1910
choreography: Fokine
music: Stravinsky

In a mysterious garden, Prince Ivan captures a magical firebird. To gain her release, she gives him one of her feathers, which will summon her back if he is ever in danger.

Into the garden comes a beautiful princess and her eleven companions, who dance with golden apples. Ivan falls in love with the princess, but is captured by the evil magician Kostchei and his monsters. Ivan calls the firebird who helps him destroy Kostchei. At last, Ivan and the princess marry and are crowned king and queen.

Petrushka
date: 1911
choreography: Fokine
music: Stravinsky

At the Butterweek Fair in old St. Petersburg, a showman sets up his booth with three puppets – the ballerina doll, the moor and a clown named Petrushka. They perform for the crowd, acting a story in which Petrushka loves the ballerina, although she prefers the moor.

Inside the booth, the puppets are living their own lives. Petrushka is cruelly treated by the showman and longs for the ballerina doll. She spurns him for the flashy moor, who beats Petrushka when he interrupts them. The crowd at the fair hears the puppets fighting. Suddenly, they burst out of the booth and the moor kills Petrushka with his scimitar. The crowd is astonished as the dying Petrushka bleeds, but the showman tells them he is only a puppet. In the end, Petrushka's ghost rises to terrify the showman.

Apollo

date: 1928
choreography: Balanchine
music: Stravinsky

Based on Greek mythology, this ballet shows the birth of the god Apollo and displays him as the leader of the three muses – Calliope the muse of poetry, Polyhymnia the muse of mime and Terpsichore the muse of dance. Terpsichore pleases Apollo the most and the ballet ends with him ascending Mount Olympus, the home of the gods, to his father Zeus.

The Prodigal Son

date: 1929
choreography: Balanchine
music: Prokofiev

Set in Biblical times, a son leaves his family intent on seeing the world with his companions. He falls in with some eerie merrymakers, who make him drunk. A siren then seduces him. Robbed of everything, he crawls home, fearing that his father will not forgive him. However, his father welcomes him home, forgiving all.

Late 20th century ballets

La Fille Mal Gardée

date: 1960
choreography: Ashton
music: Herold

Lise, the daughter of Widow Simone (who is played by a man, like a pantomime dame) is in love with a young farmer named Colas. However, her mother has grander ideas and wants her to marry Alain, the son of a rich vineyard owner. During a harvest picnic, complete with maypole dancing and clog dancing, a storm breaks out and everyone scurries indoors. The widow locks Lise in their old farmhouse, but at last the lovers manage to outwit her.

The Dream

date: 1964
choreography: Ashton
music: Mendelssohn

Based on Shakespeare's *A Midsummer Night's Dream*, this story concerns a quarrel between Oberon and Titania – the King and Queen of the Fairies.

For revenge against Titania's obsession with a little Indian boy, Oberon makes her fall in love with Bottom the weaver, who is disguised as an ass.

More comic confusion is caused when two pairs of lovers get lost in the forest. Oberon's servant, the mischievous Puck, uses magic to mix up the pairs, so that the wrong partners fall in love. At last, order is restored and everyone gets their rightful partner back.

Romeo and Juliet

date: 1965
choreography: MacMillan
music: Prokofiev

Based on Shakespeare's play, this story tells of two lovers whose families are locked into a terrible feud. Romeo and his friends gatecrash the Capulet's ball, where he falls in love with Juliet at first sight. Later that night, they swear their love to each other in the famous balcony scene. Friar Laurence marries them in secret, but a fight breaks out and Romeo's friend is killed by Juliet's cousin, Tybalt. Romeo kills Tybalt and is banished from Verona.

Meanwhile, Juliet's parents are pressing her to marry Paris. To prevent the wedding from taking place, she drinks a poison prepared by Friar Laurence, which will make her appear dead. She is buried in the family tomb and Romeo mistakenly hears that she really is dead. He returns to visit her tomb and, in despair, poisons himself. Juliet awakes and finds Romeo dead beside her. Distraught, she stabs herself.

The Taming of the Shrew

date: 1969
choreography: Cranko
music: Stolze

Based on Shakespeare's play, the story tells of two sisters, the shrew-like (bad-tempered) Kate and the younger, pretty Bianca. Bianca is courted by many men, but she cannot marry until her elder sister is wed. A poor man, Petruchio, agrees to marry Kate for money and sets about taming her temper in great comic scenes. Kate then emerges as the perfect wife.

Manon

date: 1974
choreography: MacMillan
music: Massenet

Based on an 18th century French novel, this story is about Manon – a beautiful young girl. Her beauty attracts many wealthy admirers and her brother hopes to become rich by selling her to Monsieur G.M. However, Manon falls in love with a penniless student, Des Grieux, and escapes with him.

She then changes her mind and leaves Des Grieux for the lure of wealth. She later returns to him, but Monsieur G.M. accuses her of being a prostitute and she is arrested and her brother is shot. She is deported to America, where Des Grieux finds her. They try to escape, but Manon dies in his arms.

A Month in the Country

date: 1976
choreography: Ashton
music: Chopin

Based on a play by Turgenev, the story is set in a 19th century Russian household, into which a young tutor, called Belyayev, comes to work. The lady of the house, Natalya, becomes interested in him, as do her young ward Vera and the maid Katia. The situation becomes impossible and although Belyayev loves Natalya he realizes he must leave her and never return.

Hobson's Choice

date: 1989
choreography: Bintley
music: Reade

The story tells of a selfish boot shop owner, Henry Hobson, and his three daughters. Alice and Vicky want to marry but Hobson won't let them as he uses them as unpaid assistants. The eldest daughter, Maggie, marries Will the shy bootmaker. They set up their own shop and help Alice and Vicky to get away. Hobson drinks and gets into debt, so in the end Will and Maggie take over his shop in exchange for paying his debts.

Ballet as a career

The following is a list of occupations which are available to students who have a ballet school training.

Professional ballet dancer

Most ballet school students try to gain positions performing for a professional company. However, these are not always easy to obtain, as vacancies only occur when current dancers leave.

When appointing new dancers, directors look for excellent technique, physique and stage presence. Once a contract has been won, wages and working conditions are generally good. Classes, shoes, tights and, of course, costumes are provided. Dancers' hours are regulated, but the day can be long and tiring. Those who are attached to a touring company have to get used to long periods away from home.

Promotion can come quickly – talented youngsters are often given solo opportunities within their first couple of years. However, for those who remain in the *corps de ballet*, the job can become repetitive. Experienced performers may move to smaller or experimental companies, where there may be more chance to dance a variety of roles.

Most performing careers, though, are short. Dancers rarely continue beyond their mid-thirites. Missing a year or two through injury is also common. Any extra qualifications and experience that you have will be very useful for starting a new career once your performing years are over.

Dancer in commercial theatre

Good singers who have jazz and tap experience can audition for parts in musicals that require dancers. The choreography in musicals can be very demanding, as the dance sequences are often the high point of a show.

However, life in musicals is less secure than in a ballet company. Contracts only last for the duration of the show's run, which may be short. Long running shows, though, may have several casts. Constant auditioning will become a way of life if you decide to choose this career.

Choreographer

Those who have a talent for creating dances may wish to become choreographers. Training for choreography is less well structured than training for other careers in the ballet world.

Many would-be choreographers join companies as dancers and then hope to get a creative opportunity within that company.

Others may form their own company with a group of committed dancers. They will then hope to raise funds in order to advertise and perform their work to the public, but this can be very difficult.

Dance notator

Many companies record their repertory in notation. Reading and writing these scores is a specialist job. Ideal qualities for a notator are a methodical mind, a good background in movement and dance, and a knowledge of ballet in particular.

Those who wish to become notators need to study at an organization such as the Benesh Institute or the Labanotation Institute. Once qualified, notators are in demand all over the world and may often take on the role of ballet master or mistress, or répétiteur. Some choreographers have particular notators who they prefer to work with. As a choreographer's assistant, a notator may be expected to help restage old ballets.

Ballet teacher

For those who can communicate well and who are interested in helping the next generation of dancers, teaching may be a good option.

A teacher training course will equip you with the skills to pass on the Classical technique and the love of dancing to others. At the same time, you will be perfecting your own technique and studying subjects such as music, anatomy and child development. Training usually takes three years, but many dance colleges provide a one year course for ex-professional dancers.

Education officer

Many theatres and all ballet companies have education departments. A job as an education officer involves varied work, dealing with the public and often with school children.

Education officers promote an understanding of dance to the public. They do this by devising projects; running workshops and preparing information packs and videos. They also present lecture demonstrations and take part in residencies, when they go into schools or colleges to help students create and present a performance.

Those who work in this field often have an academic dance background, having studied for a dance degree. Others, though, may have been students at ballet school and ex-professional dancers.

What do ex-dancers do?

An obvious choice for an ex-dancer is to take a non-performing role within a company, by becoming a teacher, répétiteur, notator, choreographer or ballet master/mistress.

Many ex-dancers retrain for a new career within ballet or the arts, such as administration, public relations, making films, stage management or special effects makeup. Others begin an entirely different career, such as physiotherapy, law or even truck driving. New jobs may involve retraining or going back to college and studying for new qualifications.

Studying dance

If you don't want to take up ballet training, you could study for a dance degree, which combines practical skills with academic study. Dance can be studied on its own or with another subject, such as drama.

Dance can also form part of a general teaching degree. In many schools dance is an important part of the school curriculum, especially for young children. At postgraduate level, dance students may undertake historical research and help with reconstructing original choreography.

Ballet websites

If you have access to the Internet, you can visit these websites to find out more about ballet. For links to these sites, go to the Usborne Quicklinks Website at **www.usborne-quicklinks.com** and enter the keyword "ballet".

Internet safety

When using the Internet, please follow the Internet safety guidelines shown on the Usborne Quicklinks Website. If you write a message in a website guest book or on a message board, do not include any personal information such as your full name, address or telephone number, and ask an adult before you give your email address. Never arrange to meet anyone you have talked to on the Internet.

The websites described in this book are regularly reviewed and the links in Usborne Quicklinks are updated. However, the content of a website may change at any time and Usborne Publishing is not responsible for the content on any website other than its own. We recommend that children are supervised while on the Internet, that they do not use Internet chat rooms, and that Internet filtering software is used to block unsuitable material.

General sites

Website 1
The place to go for UK ballet fans. Get the latest news on companies and performances; read interviews, reviews and biographies of dancers past and present (with photos); read regular columns by choreographers or sift through past online magazine issues.

Website 2
Find out more about ballet history and technique; read profiles of some of the most important people in the world of dance, past and present; explore rare photo archives and listen to clips of ballet music.

Website 3
A site with lots of information on the different aspects of ballet - the stages in putting on a performance, the life of a dancer, ballet history and technique.

Website 4
This site includes an illustrated beginner's guide to ballet to print out and keep. There is also information on life behind the scenes in a ballet company; there are e-cards to send, instructions on how to make your own tutu, and, for the young, pictures to print out and colour in.

Website 5
Visit this site for in-depth background information on ballets, choreographers and composers. You can also do quizzes and wordsearches.

Website 6
A detailed account of ballet through the centuries with lots of photos to bring the history alive.

Website 7
An interactive, audio-visual timeline on the history of ballet, showing its development over the past 500 years.

Website 8
A site which explores the connection between ballet and other art forms: painting, sculpture, film, drama, architecture and music.

Website 9
An explanation of the science behind classical dance - how dancers bend, jump and spin, and how they sense what it is they are doing.

Website 10
Advice from a dance expert on a variety of topics, including healthy eating, avoiding injury, passing auditions and getting into choreography.

Website 11
Read ballet news, articles and interviews, and see video clips.

Website 12
A virtual theatre with dance information and fun things to do for the young - listen to instruments, dress up dancers, and more.

Website 13
Another site for the young, with ballet stories and puzzles.

Improve your technique

Website 1
Find inspiration for your own dancing with the American Ballet Theatre's online dictionary where you can watch video clips of professional dancers demonstrating different steps and improve your knowledge and pronunciation of ballet terms.

Website 2
More inspiration from this selection of video clips - Pennsylvania Ballet dancers demonstrate steps to music.

Website 3
Detailed tips by a principal dancer who now teaches ballet, on taking *barre*, learning the *plié* and *pirouettes,* and on doing floor exercises.

Website 4
Photographs of basic ballet positions for young beginners.

Website 5
Listen to clips of music used for ballet classes.

Website 6
More music clips used for ballet steps.

Website 7
Instruction on technique from basic steps to advanced turns.

Website 8
Computer-generated simulations of some of the most advanced ballet steps.

For photos and clipart

Website 1
A large collection of general ballet photos to look at.

Website 2
View photos, paintings, drawings and sculpture at this site.

Website 3
Ballet art work and photos, including pastel pictures and stained glass.

Website 4
Large collection of ballet photos, mainly of the Ballet San Jose Silicon Valley.

Website 5
A selection of ballet photos, some in black and white.

Website 6
A photo collection of famous ballerinas.

Website 7
Paintings of ballet dancers by the French Impressionist Edgar Dégas.

Website 8
An interactive look at Dégas paintings for the very young.

Website 9
Ballet paintings by the artist Valery Kosorukov, sometimes referred to as the Russian Dégas.

Website 10
Pictures of ballet backdrops, some from the Ballet Russe de Monte Carlo, and designed by famous artists.

Website 11
Send an e-card. You can choose from a selection of photos of ballet dancers in different natural settings.

Dance magazines

You usually have to pay to view all of a magazine but there are often sections that you can look at free.

Website 1
A newsletter covering the world of classical ballet mainly in the USA, with information on dancers, companies and performances.

Website 2
Selected articles in a monthly online magazine, with the latest ballet news and special web exclusives.

Website 3
A selection of ballet news and reviews written for young dancers, with competitions.

Website 4
The latest ballet and dance news, with photos, reviews, features, interviews and links to recommended sites.

Ballet companies

The best way to find out about a ballet company is to visit its website where you will find news of the company's forthcoming performances, how to book tickets, biographies of the dancers, details of the repertory, and history of the company. In most cases, there are also photo galleries of dancers and performances. Below is a selection of ballet companies. To find more companies, visit the recommended sites under "Links to other websites" on this page.

Website 1
The Albany Berkshire Ballet, USA.

Website 2
American Ballet Theatre (ABT). Includes an interactive dictionary with video clips.

Website 3
Atlanta Ballet, USA.

Website 4
The Australian Ballet. Has lots of information on life behind the scenes.

Website 5
The Birmingham Royal Ballet, UK. Includes ballet story synopses.

Website 6
The official site of the Bolshoi Theatre, home of the Bolshoi Ballet.

Website 7
A photo-essay on the Bolshoi after the collapse of the USSR.

Website 8
Cwmni Ballet Gwent (Wales).

Website 9
Dance Theatre of Harlem.

Website 10
The English National Ballet.

Website 11
Hamburg Ballet.

Website 12
The Kirov Ballet.

Website 13
Take a virtual tour of the Maryinsky Theatre, home of the Kirov Ballet.

Website 14
Biographies of both Kirov and Bolshoi dancers.

Website 15
The National Ballet of Canada. Includes lots of general information on ballet and fun things to do.

Website 16
New Adventures, formerly called Adventures in Motion Pictures (AMP), who produce unique interpretations of ballets such as Swan Lake.

Website 17
New York City Ballet. Includes music clips.

Website 18
Northern Ballet Theatre, UK.

Website 19
Paris Opéra Ballet.

Website 20
Pennsylvania Ballet. Includes video clips to music.

Website 21
The Royal Ballet, UK.

Website 22
The Royal Danish Ballet.

Website 23
Scottish Ballet.

Website 24
Stuttgart Ballet.

Links to other websites

Website 1
An enormous list of links to ballet and dance sites.

Website 2
International list of links for dancers, organized by category, on a wide range of topics.

Website 3
Lots of dance and ballet links, to companies, funding organizations, schools and much more.

Website 4
Links to ballet and dance companies around the world.

Glossary

Abstract ballets. Ballets which have no story or theme, but which display the dancers' skills for their own sake.

Adage. From an Italian musical term which means at ease. *Adage* steps are slow and sustained, as one position flows into another.

Allegro. An Italian musical term which means quick and lively. In ballet, *allegro* steps are fast.

Arabesque. A type of *adage* step, in which you balance on one leg with the other stretched out behind you.

Attitude. A position in which you stand on one leg, lifting and curving the other leg around you.

Backcloth. A large cloth hanging down at the back of the stage on which scenery is painted.

Barre. A wooden handrail that runs around ballet studios, which helps dancers to balance when they are doing warm-up exercises.

Benesh notation. A system of dance notation developed by Rudolf and Joan Benesh in 1955.

Centre work. Exercises performed in the middle of the studio to improve balance and control.

Character role. A role in a ballet which requires a great deal of acting, rather than dancing ability.

Choreography. The arrangement of step combinations in any dance performance.

Classical ballets. A group of Russian story ballets, such as *Swan Lake*, created in the late 19th century. The term is also used to describe any ballet created during this period.

Contemporary dance. A modern dance style, which is less rigid in structure than Classical ballet.

Corps de ballet. Dancers in a ballet company who perform the group dances and do not usually dance leading roles.

Divertissement. A sequence of dances that show off the dancer's skill, rather than contribute to the ballet's story.

Elevation. The height of a jump.

Enchainement. A series of steps linked together to make a sequence.

Front cloth. A large cloth which comes down in front of the scenery, while it is being changed during a performance.

Labanotation. A system of dance notation originated by Rudolf von Laban in the 1920s.

Line. The flowing shapes that a dancer's body makes.

Modern ballet. Any ballet that has been created in the last half of the 20th century.

National dances. Traditional folk dances from countries around the world. Versions of these are included in some ballets and are called character dances.

Notation. Systems of signs, such as Benesh Notation and Labanotation, which are used to record ballet steps on paper.

On *pointe*. Dancing on the very tips of your toes, with help from stiffened shoes, called *pointe* shoes. Usually, only females dance on *pointe*.

Opposition. The state in most jumps where the opposite arm to the leading leg is lifted or pointed out in front.

Pas de deux. A dance sequence within a ballet, performed by a male and a female together, also called a duet.

Physiotherapist. A person who is trained to treat the muscle injuries of dancers and other athletes.

Pirouette. A turning step.

Placement. The correct positioning of one part of your body in relation to another.

Positions of the arms. Eight different ways of standing and holding your arms.

Positions of the feet. Five different ways in which your weight is evenly distributed over your feet, whatever position your body is in.

Posture. The way you hold your body when you stand, sit or move.

Props. The pieces of equipment that dancers or actors use on stage, such as the spindles in *The Sleeping Beauty*, which help to tell the story.

Repertory. The collection of ballets that a company performs regularly, also known by the French term *repertoire*.

Romantic ballets. Ballets that were created in the early 19th century and which were influenced by the Romantic movement in art.

Rosin. A yellow crystal which breaks down into a white powder that dancers rub onto their shoes to stop them from slipping.

Scenario. A written outline of what happens on stage during a ballet.

Set. The scenery and props on stage.

Spotting. The trick of always looking at the same spot when you are turning, to stop you from feeling dizzy.

Technique. The defined steps in ballet and the style in which they are performed.

Theme ballets. Ballets which do not have a story, but communicate a particular mood or idea to the audience instead.

Torso. The middle of the body, not including arms, legs, head or neck.

Turn-out. The way in which the dancer's legs are turned out from the hip in ballet technique.

Pronouncing French terms

The following list shows how to pronounce the French terms that appear in this book.

arabesque à terre - arab-esk a tair
arabesque en l'air - arab-esk on lair
arabesque penchée - arab-esk pon-shay
assemblé derrière - ass-om-blay dare-ee-air
attitude - at-ee-tood

barre - bar
bas - bah
battements fondus - bat-a-mon fon-doo
battements frappés - bat-a-mon frap-ay
battements tendus - bat-a-mon ton-doo
batterie - bat-er-ree
bourrée piqué - boo-ray pee-kay
bras - bra

changement - shonsh-mon
corps - cor
coryphées - cor-ee-fay
croisé - kwa-zay

demi - dem-ee
développé - day-vel-oh-pay
divertissements - dee-ver-tees-mon

écarté - ay-car-tay
échappé sauté - ay-sha-pay so-tay
éffacé - ay-fass-ay
en cinquième - on sank-ee-em
en croix - on kwa
en dedans - on der-don
en dehors - on der-or
en face - on fass
en première - on prem-ee-air
en quatrième - on ka-tree-em
en seconde - on ser-gond
en troisième - on twa-see-em
enchainement - on-shain-mon
entrechat quatre - on-tre-sha ka-tra

glissade derrière - gliss-ard der-ee-air
grand battements - gron bat-a-mon
grand jeté en avant - gron shet-ay on a-von
grand plié - gron plee-ay

ouvert - oo-vairt

pas de chat - pah der sha
pas de deux - pah der de
pas de trois - pah der twa
plié - plee-ay
pointe - point (this word is pronounced as in English, though it has a French spelling)
ports de bras - por der bra

relevé - re-lev-ay
ronds de jambe à terre - rond de shomb a tair

sissonne fermé en avant - siss-on fair-may on a-von

tableau - tab-low
temps de poisson - ton de pwa-son

Acknowledgments

The publishers would like to thank the following for help with producing this book:

Sir Peter Wright (Director); Michael Clifford (Shoe Supervisor); Desmond Kelly (Assistant Director); Lili Sobieralska (Wardrobe Mistress) and Michelle Wong (Education Officer) of The Birmingham Royal Ballet for their advice and assistance.
Charles H Fox Ltd, Covent Garden, London for supplying items of make-up on page 25.
Freed of London Ltd for supplying shoes on pages 16-17.
Mr A J G Howse FRCS for providing reference material for page 35.
Hilary Kerridge for making the leotards on pages 34-51.
Vanessa Palmer of The Royal Ballet for modelling on page 37.

The photographs in this book are reproduced by courtesy of the following:

Board of Trustees, Victoria & Albert Museum (23, bottom left).
Bill Cooper (3, bottom; 6, top left, middle, bottom right; 7, middle; 9, left; 10, top right, bottom left, middle right, first and third bottom right; 12, top left; 13, right, bottom left; 14, top right, middle, bottom right; 20, bottom left, bottom right; 21; 22; 23, top left, middle right, bottom right; 24, top, middle; 26, top left; 27).
Anthony Crickmay (2, main photo; 4; 5, top right, bottom right; 8, left, top right; 11, left; 12, left; 14, middle left; 15, right; 18, top right; 19, middle right; 30, photo of Francesca Filpi and Rebecca Weekes).
Jim Fraser (23, top right; 28; 29).
Hulton Deutsch (52, top).
Camilla Jessell (31).
Kobal Collection (20, top right).
Dennis Leigh (20, top left).
Chris Nash (9, right).
Northern Ballet Theatre (5, bottom left).
Performing Arts Library/Clive Barda (6, bottom left, top right).
Performing Arts Library/Laurie Lewis (53, bottom).
Royal Academy of Dancing (32).
Royal Opera House (12, bottom, right).
Angela Taylor (5, top left; 10, top left, second and fourth bottom right; 11, top right; 14, top left, bottom left; 15, left; 19, top right, 20, middle; 24, bottom; 26, top right; 52, bottom).
Theatre Museum, Victoria & Albert Museum (2, top; 8, bottom right; 13, top left; 18, middle left; 19, left; 33; 53, top).
Alan Wood (16, top right).

Cover photograph: © Eric Richmond/ArenaPAL; dancers from English National Ballet in *Cinderella*.

Index

First published in 1994 by Usborne Publishing Ltd, Usborne House, 83-85 Saffron Hill, London, EC1N 8RT, England. www.usborne.com
Copyright © 2005, 2000, 1994 Usborne Publishing Ltd.
The name Usborne and the devices ♀ ⊕ are Trade Marks of Usborne Publishing Ltd.

Printed in Spain.